W9-BXE-764

# THE MINISTER'S COMPLETE GUIDE TO SUCCESSFUL RETIREMENT

# THE MINISTER'S COMPLETE GUIDE TO SUCCESSFUL RETIREMENT

*by*

*Norman Lobsenz*

CHANNEL PRESS, INC.
*Great Neck, New York*

Published in October, 1955, by Channel Press, Inc., 159 Northern Boulevard, Great Neck, New York

Manufactured in the United States of America by
The Haddon Craftsmen, Inc., Scranton, Pennsylvania

## *ACKNOWLEDGMENTS*

*Thanks are due the following firms and individuals for their kind permission to quote from their copyrighted works, as detailed below:*

INTRODUCTION: Eugene Friedman and Robert J. Havighurst, authors of *The Meaning of Work and Retirement,* published by the University of Chicago Press, Chicago, Illinois. Copyright, 1954, by The University of Chicago.

CHAPTER ONE: Nolan B. Harmon, author of *Ministerial Ethics and Etiquette,* published by Abingdon Press, Nashville, Tennessee. Copyright, 1928, by Lamar and Whitmore; and 1950, by Pierce and Smith.

Walter E. Schuette, author of *The Minister's Personal Guide,* published by Harper & Brothers. Copyright, 1953, by Harper & Brothers.

CHAPTER THREE: Frank Scribner, for material from his article in the November, 1949, issue of *Advance,* published by the Congregational Christian Churches.

CHAPTER SEVEN: Maxwell Lehman and Morton Yarmon, for material quoted from an article in the July, 1952, issue of *Lifetime Living* Magazine, copyright 1952, by *Lifetime Living.* This excellent monthly is now The Journal of Lifetime Living.

CHAPTER EIGHT: The Board of Pensions of The Presbyterian Church in the United States of America, for an article in *Monday Morning* Magazine, published biweekly in Philadelphia, Pennsylvania; the July 1955, issue.

CHAPTER NINE: Kenneth L. Wilson, for his article on Penney Farms, appearing in the July, 1952, issue of *Lifetime Living* Magazine, copyright 1952, by *Lifetime Living.*

The University of Michigan Press, Ann Arbor, Michigan, publishers of *Housing the Aging,* a report on a seminar on this subject, edited by Wilma T. Donahue. (Page 251.) Copyright 1954, by the University of Michigan.

CHAPTER TEN: Mort Weisinger, author of *1001 Valuable Things You Can Get Free,* published by Bantam Books, Inc., New York City, New York, in a paperbound edition, and Grosset and Dunlap, Inc., New York City, New York, in a hard-cover edition. Copyright, 1955, by Bantam Books, Inc.

CHAPTER ELEVEN: The Metropolitan Life Insurance Company, New York City, New York, publishers of *Your Future and You,* one of an excellent series of pamphlets on health available without charge. Copyright, 1954, by Metropolitan Life.

CHAPTER TWELVE: The University of Michigan Press, Ann Arbor, Michigan, publishers of *Housing the Aging,* a report on a seminar on this subject, edited by Wilma T. Donahue. (Page 234.) Copyright, 1954, by the University of Michigan.

APPENDIX: Section One, a national pollen index, is based on a valuable survey made by Oren C. Durham, Pollen Survey Committee, American Academy of Allergy; Chief Botanist, Abbott Laboratories, North Chicago, Illinois.

Section Two, a report on tax problems, is based on material from *The Minister's Federal Income Tax Guide,* published annually by Doniger & Raughley, Inc., Great Neck, New York.

# TABLE OF CONTENTS

# INTRODUCTION

This is going to be a straight-from-the-shoulder book about the problems of your retirement from the ministry. It will, I hope, be helpful as it examines and advises on the financial, emotional, geographical, physical, and spiritual aspects of retirement. Its aim is to show you how to get the most out of your later years. It will not, I promise, be namby-pamby.

Too many observations on retirement are made through those familiar, proverbial rose-colored glasses. Too often retirement is seen as the "golden sunset of life"; and too seldom are the late afternoon thunderclouds noticed or mentioned.

Let us face facts squarely. The later years are likely to have more than their quota of thunderclouds. Despite the great strides mankind has taken in making life healthier and happier for older persons, the pitfalls of the retirement years are still legion.

Earning power is curtailed. Health and strength weaken; friends drop away; family life grows more tenuous; work is denied to persons over certain age limits; one finds it increasingly difficult to develop new interests, new avocations, and new horizons.

Such are the pitfalls of retirement years for the average

person. And let us be blunt again—these pifalls are likely to exist in even more pernicious form for the retired minister!

His income, rarely high enough during his working life to enable him to save a substantial backlog of money, drops off to virtual nothingness. His pension is small, and even when supplemented by the Social Security payments he is newly entitled to, makes a total income which rarely rises above subsistence level.

He must find new housing, for the parsonages he has occupied during his working life are now lived in by others. And since he has rarely had a chance to put together enough money over the years to buy or build his own home, he must start from scratch to seek a place in which to live. And then he must furnish it, again from "scratch."

In most cases he must settle in a new location, for experts in ministerial etiquette and psychology advise a retiring minister to sever himself as much as possible from his former congregation. This in turn means many old friendships disrupted.

Because the pressure of work on a minister is so great and so constant, few ministers have the time or energy to develop hobbies or avocations which can contribute to their income or stimulate their mental life after retirement.

And these are merely a few of the general problems faced by the retired minister. In addition, he has unique *pyscho-logical* problems to face and overcome. For example:

Virtually overnight his status changes from that of a man who has been a community leader, a focus of action, an individual and symbol needed by many people—into that of a man who is no longer needed by anybody. Retirement not only removes the minister from the center of the stage, but it is likely to take him off the stage entirely.

Says Dr. John Scotford, who served as representative of the Home Mission Board of the Congregational Christian

Churches for many years: "A chief danger for the retired minister is that he will feel himself to be a forgotten man. At one time I used to travel about the country and take pictures of retired ministers for publicity purposes. Actually, the good this did for their morale was much more important than any publicity results gained."

Another minister, pointing up a second problem, told me: "It's awfully hard for a minister to take the Gospel idea of humility seriously. During his career he has had the praise of his congregation and of the public at large. Unless he has learned to take this praise in his stride—and with many a grain of salt—he is likely to feel that retirement is taking the leaven out of his life."

Further, ministers have always been the master of time: engrossed by, and indeed in many cases pushed into a score of different activities, they never have lacked for "something to do next." More often the minister lacks for time to do it in. But with retirement, this situation changes with startling and frightening suddenness. Now, Time is the master; now, Time must be filled and must be "spent." And the sudden lack of imperative things to do may loom like a nightmare unless a man has fortified himself with inner stamina and outside interests.

The ministerial profession heightens one more problem common to most retiring men—that of finding a new identification in life after the identification provided by one's work is gone.

As Sociologists Eugene Friedman and Robert J. Havighurst point out in their book, *The Meaning of Work and Retirement* (University of Chicago), a man's work is more than merely a time-filling or income-producing activity. It's a purposeful activity which affects the whole range of his participation in society. And that part of his life which is not spent working is nevertheless deeply affected by the kind of work he does and the manner in which he does it. *The job is the axis of a man's life pattern,* determining in large part the nature of his experiences and the depth of his satisfaction.

If we have emphasized the difficulties and dangers of retirement, we have done so chiefly to bring home the fact that retirement is a stage of life which must be studied, planned for and guided just as assiduously as youth, adolescence and maturity. It will be the objective of this book to provide you with as much helpful information as possible to help you plan wisely for your retirement.

And so let's not overlook the many positive aspects of the problem. For one thing, the United States population includes a greater number of older persons today than ever before; and their numbers will grow. Strides in medical science are giving more of us a longer life expectancy, and making our older years healthier ones.

A recent U.S. Labor Department survey on the status of older men and women shows that there are now 12,500,000 persons in the United States sixty-five years or older. But by 1970—according to conservative estimates —there will be *twenty* million people over sixty-five, and slightly more than 60,000,000 men and women over the age of forty-five.

What does this all mean to you?

Well, it means that more and more attention is being paid to the problems of older persons and to the problems of retirement. An ever-increasing number of books, magazine articles, surveys, research projects, and scientific investigations are focusing on the subject. Out of this is bound to come new conditions and techniques to help make your retirement years more productive and happier.

And, if a minister is handicapped with more complex retirement problems than most people, he also has one tremendous advantage: his faith.

A recent annual meeting of the Gerontological Society

of America was told that the two major prerequisites for making a good adjustment to retirement and to old age are: (1) hard work over long hours of time; and (2), a religion-oriented life. Certainly the minister qualifies on both these counts!

Adjustment to retirement is, after all, a matter of personality and individuality. Just as each man will gauge retirement advice and make his retirement decisions on the basis of his own needs and judgment, so will he make his overall adjustment on the basis of his own character.

This is true because, basically, retirement is a state of mind. If you can make your approach, your state of mind, a positive one—if you can look ahead to retirement as a period for new achievements and a new kind of happiness—you will be able to rise above its perils.

# THE MINISTER'S COMPLETE GUIDE TO SUCCESSFUL RETIREMENT

*Chapter One*

# HOW TO LEAVE YOUR CONGREGATION GRACEFULLY

All men, in their lives, face "moments of truth" —times when the uncompromising realities of life rush headlong at them to test their spiritual or physical mettle. The phrase was coined to pinpoint that lightning-fast instant in a bullfight when the bull charges at the poised matador. But it applies equally well to the soldier at H-hour; to the statesman faced with deliberations of war or peace; to the man who has just been told he has an inoperable cancer.

Ministers come face to face with many "moments of truth" during their lives. Indeed, their trials and tests begin with the very first stirrings of the call to the ministry itself, and endure and recur throughout long years of service. Nor is it only in their own lives that ministers must stand firm and resolute at crucial moments of decision; again and again they become intensely involved, as counselor or guide, as they work with some member of the congregation whose affairs have reached a crisis.

But the "moment of truth" that the minister is perhaps most reluctant to face is the moment of his own retirement. It is the time when he needs all his courage and spiritual resources to face one of life's ultimate facts.

Few men and women can handle partings with equanimity. I know one hard-headed, successful businessman who has made it a rule that neither his wife nor children may be present at the railroad station or airport to see him off when he leaves on a business trip.

"I simply can't stand the good-byes, the last-minute reminders, and the waiting around for the plane to load or the train to start moving," he told me. "Why do people insist on making leave-takings so painful?"

Yes, any parting of the ways is difficult; and one of the most painful leave-takings in existence occurs when a minister retires from his parish. There are few fields of endeavor in which a man's ties with his work are so close, so interwoven with every aspect of his twenty-four-hour-a-day living, so involved with his spiritual happiness, so merged with his personal friendships, and so intimate a part of his very way of life.

Yet at the same time, there are few leave-takings which must be made so sharply, so cleanly, and so irrevocably.

You know the reasons, of course. At stake is the continuing welfare of your congregation and its relationship with the new pastor. Both he and they must be free to work out an intimate association without any interference on your part—whether it be passive or active, well-meaning or not, deliberate or accidental.

A retirement is first of all a separation. You can make it sticky and messy and long-drawn-out, like a gob of taffy being pulled in half. Or you can make it quick and neat, so that all concerned are free in spirit and fact to go about their next bit of business.

*This graceful retirement from your post can be one of the most important services you will ever perform for your congregation!*

There are two elements to the problem of retirement. One is *when* to retire; the other is *how* to do it. And because the decision on when to retire is one that must be made for reasons which vary widely in each individual case, there is little point in discussing the problem here at length. No one can lay down even broad and general suggestions for a matter resting on such intensely personal factors.

Yet all pastorates do end! As Dr. Scotford, writing in *Protestant Church Administration and Equipment,* declared:

"Like death and taxes, the farewell sermon is inevitable. But ministers are afraid of resigning. Part of their fear stems from aversion to change, which often increases with the years. As we grow older we hesitate to face new adjustments . . .

"For some men, the fear of resigning is a financial fear . . . Others are reluctant to face the fact that the years have crept up upon them, and that they are older than they like to admit. Some just do not know what to do with themselves when there are no longer calls to be made and sermons to be prepared. Rare is the man who can face his own resignation in an optimistic mood."

How then—despite all the turmoil in one's own heart—can this leave-taking be handled for the best interests of all concerned? What method will benefit the retiring minister himself . . . the new minister . . . and the congregation?

Here now are nine suggestions on both an ethical and a practical level:

*1. Start the wheels of retirement turning yourself.* The job of making the decision on your retirement must be yours alone; it must never wait upon embarrassing nudges from your superiors or your congregation.

*2. Until your decision to retire is an accomplished fact, do not consult anyone or seek "outside opinions."* Raising the question within your own congregation, even though you may limit your discussions to a few church members, often has a tendency to create more problems than it solves.

"Some people in the congregation," Dr. Scotford continues, "will urge a minister to stay on simply because they imagine that to do otherwise would be an 'unfriendly act' on their part . . . If a minister wants to hear a lot of flattering but insincere words, let him ask the first dozen members whom he encounters whether he should leave or not.

"A wise pastor will not even *suggest* the possibility that he may depart until his mind is made up—and then he will not reconsider his decision."

*3. Don't permit yourself the emotional luxury of a "farewell" sermon.* There are instances of ministers who have taken advantage of their imminent departure to "get tough," perhaps for the first time, with those in their congregation who have not always seen eye to eye with them. There are other ministers who give way to the temptation to deliver a eulogy to themselves, disguising it only slightly as a "summing-up of their career and achievements." There are still other ministers who fall victim to their own emotions and deliver a frankly sentimental valedictory. It is not a difficult thing to turn a chapel into a vale of tears—but what good does it do in this situation?

Basically, none of these approaches are useful. And certainly, none of them are graceful!

One minister states that your last sermon should simply be the best Gospel sermon you have ever preached. That in itself will do more to enhance your memory in the minds of your congregation than any sentimental good-bye from the pulpit.

*4. Make every effort to see to it that the new minister gets a warm greeting, and that the congregation is prepared to welcome him with friendliness and enthu-*

*siasm*. The way in which you do this will not only have a lasting effect on the future welfare of your successor, but on the congregation you are leaving as well.

If you express or even imply doubts about your successor's abilities, you create an atmosphere of suspicion, distrust, and possibly even outright discord. But if you commend the new pastor to your congregation with sincerity, they can work together from the very start with assurances of success.

5. *Get out of the church, out of the parish, and out of town—before your successor arrives.* This may seem harsh advice, but it is the most important single thing you can do for the benefit of all concerned. "No minister," says Nolan B. Harmon in his excellent book, *Ministerial Ethics and Etiquette* (Abingdon Press, Nashville, Tennessee), "should be constantly going back to gossip with the brethren or hear comments on the work of his successor . . . Although the latter may not admit it, the presence of the former pastor will be embarrassing to the new man."

In *The Minister's Personal Guide,* Dr. Walter E. Schuette makes this point with even greater emphasis. Says this well-known author, who at one time supervised the affairs of over two hundred Ohio churches:

"When the retired minister remains within the area of the last church served, what a thorn in the flesh he can be for his successor! . . . He still has many friends . . . Their readiness to champion him cannot fail to hurt the new minister. The new minister is made to feel like an intruder.

"When individual official acts are required, as for marriages and funerals, the old minister is asked to officiate solo or to have an honored share in the ceremonies. He is consulted on all sorts of questions, the decisions of which in truth belong to the new minister. When the new minister displeases members . . . the grievance is carried to the retired pastor. . . .

"This is where the need of abundant grace becomes evident: grace enough to move the retired minister to say, 'He is your pastor, I am not.' "

Yes, despite the closeness of the ties between parishioner and retired minister, they must be broken to preserve the relationship of the congregation to the church. That is why a retired minister must move away; or, when he cannot move, that is why he must make his congregation understand definitely and firmly that he is no longer their pastor, in fact as well as in name.

*6. Don't undertake to "fill in" the new man on the peculiarities of your congregation.* This is an entirely gratuitous chore; it serves no purpose. There is no need to warn a new man about various members of the congregation, since he will learn their foibles and idiosyncrasies soon enough for himself. Moreover, since individuals differ, it is possible and even probable that he and they will react upon each other quite differently than the way in which you and the congregation affected each other during your service in the same church.

If you are going to have any contact at all with your successor, you can be helpful to him by filling him in on the facts—*facts, not opinions!*—with which he will have to deal in his new parish. I know of no man in any field of endeavor who will not benefit from a friendly summary of local conditions and procedures when he begins a new job.

Although a minister may feel obligated to supply such helpful information to his successor, he should exercise great care not to appear to be directing future work in any way. "One may advise and state methods previously followed," says Nolan Harmon, "but the minister of tact will know how to make it clear that the situation is now entirely in the hands of the new man."

*7. Leave your parish in good order, both so far as church property and your personal affairs are concerned.* Parish records should be correct and up-to-date. And the rectory should be made ready for its new occupant. There is never any excuse for sloppiness or slovenliness in either of these two areas.

Similarly, you must take great pains to clear any personal debts—even small bills at local stores. Ministers often have difficulty in making ends meet; often they rely during pressed periods on the credit they receive from neighborhood retailers. The only way to be sure that you overlook no bill, forget no debt and leave no petty and annoying heritage of nagging monthly statements, is to *clean your slate before you retire.*

*8. "Remember that you can't go home again."* Thomas Wolfe said this in a powerful novel, meaning that it is indeed impossible for a man to recapture his past. Yet in their own way, some retired ministers do hope to "go home again," figuratively if not literally, by keeping in touch with their former parishioners. To do so not only arouses questions of ministerial etiquette; it also prolongs the bitter-sweetness of parting, and prevents the retired minister from turning resolutely forward toward his own new life.

More often than not it is the parishioner, not the minister, who causes this painful and complex problem. For even if the pastor has conquered himself to the extent that he avoids making any comments on parish affairs, he may still be asked by old friends to perform a marriage ceremony for a daughter; he may yet be begged to baptize a baby, or to say a few words at the funeral of an older person who looked to him for spiritual guidance through many years.

Tempting as these requests may be, flattering as they may be, the wise minister finds a way to say a kindly "no, thank you." Only harm and recriminations can follow if instead he continues to officiate at church rituals for a favored few in his former congregation. This does not mean that he must end his friendships; a tactful man can learn how to continue to be a friend even if he does not serve as pastor.

In those exceptional cases when a parishioner feels that his former pastor "must" officiate, matters can be handled gracefully if the request is made, *with explanations,* through the present minister. If the family fails to do this, the retired minister can gently show them the questions of courtesy involved, and suggest that they make the approach through proper channels. Often both ministers can play a part in the actual ceremony.

It is important that the retired minister should be careful, even in his secular relationships, not to seem to be intruding into his former congregation. Letters, anniversary and holiday greetings and the like should be kept to a minimum, or restricted to old personal friends. Visits should be few and far between. And in no case should a visit or a letter be a pathway to involvement in parish affairs.

*9.* There is one more bit of etiquete the retired minister should observe before he can congratulate himself on a truly graceful leave-taking of his congregation. And that is—*he must stay out of the affairs of the new parish in which he lives.*

You may think of yourself as a veteran, as an elder statesman; but the minister who now welcomes you in his congregation is not necessarily going to look kindly upon a flow of unsolicited advice or well-meaning meddling. And even the fellow-members of your new congregation do not want to hear how you did things in your former parish. No people with any pride in their own undertaking can enjoy hearing unfavorable comparisons.

After reading this you may say to yourself, "Does this mean that after my retirement my life must become meaningless and empty?"

The answer, most decidedly, is "Not at all!" To the minister who knows how to retire successfully, life can be fuller and more meaningful than ever before. The very depth of his experience and background enables him to bring more, much more to his own world and to the worlds of those about him.

Other chapters in this book will, I hope, point out ways for you to do this. But do not start your retirement with a feeling of futility. Do not succumb to that hollow sense of void and failure which some ministers feel when taking leave of their last congregation. Think how terribly unfair they are being to themselves!

Instead, say to yourself that your job is done; that you have truly accomplished something worthwhile; and that you face the future with no regrets.

*Chapter Two*

# MINISTERS LOOK AT RETIREMENT PLANNING

Planning in advance is one of the keys to a happy and successful retirement. So many conflicting possibilities, so many alternatives, and so many decisions arise, that it is completely unrealistic to leave them to the mood of the moment. Let me challenge you. Let me ask if right now you *know*:

·how to save or invest wisely for future income;

·how to earn extra money after retirement;

·how to select insurance coverage that will give you worry-free protection;

·how to budget your living expenses after retirement;

·how to occupy your mind, and reinvigorate your body with new interests and activities;

·how to remain as healthy as possible;

·how to adjust to retirement with your wife, your family, and your friends;

·where to live—in what locality and in what kind of living accommodation.

These are not questions to be ignored; nor are they problems to be resolved lightly or quickly. A man should devote a good part of his *pre-retirement* years to defining his personal concept of retirement; to getting all the facts and reviewing them with an open mind; and to making his plans on the basis of these facts, plus his needs and wants.

In order to dig out each important factor to be considered by men contemplating retirement from the active ministry, the publishers and author of this book embarked on a two-pronged research program. First, we devised a questionnaire and sent it to retired ministers to get the benefit of their thinking and experience.

Second, we wrote to active ministers whose congregations seemed likely to include greater-than-average numbers of retired ministers; and we asked what *they* had learned about various aspects of the retirement problem.

The splendid cooperation received on both these surveys emphasized the importance of the topic of this book; and we would like to take a moment here and now to express our deep gratitude to all those ministers—retired and active—who so wholeheartedly gave of their time and advice.

Because he lives in a "retirement city" famous for the number of older folks it attracts, Dr. Aaron N. Meckel, pastor of the First Congregational Church in St. Petersburg, Florida, was able to give us a comprehensive picture. Here is what he says:

> From my experience, some of the main things to be borne in mind by men contemplating retirement from the active ministry would seem to be these:
>
> (1) It is advisable for the retired clergyman to plan on becoming a *working* member of a specific church, preferably of his own denomination. This is far better than trying to be 'all things to all men.' We have a number of retired clergymen serving effectively on various boards and committees of our church. Fortunately, they are not dictatorial or hard-headed but pliable and emotionally flexible in spirit.
>
> (2) A retired minister should plan to participate

in local ministers' groups and associations. This serves two purposes: it helps him feel he is not completely out of touch with his life's work; and it may open up opportunities for pulpit supply work.

(3) All of us must plan to learn to live within our physical limitations, and to live there with a smile. We must accept *ourselves.* If we do, we become a blessing and a benediction by our presence alone. And that is saying a lot.

(4) Insofar as possible, one should plan to make sure of an adequate post-retirement income. Pensions, annuities, Social Security, and the possibilities of part-time employment should all be carefully studied beforehand, and—with the aid of a financial adviser, if necessary—worked into an overall financial program.

(5) The main thing is to plan to keep mentally alive and spiritually growing.

Now for the results of our questionnaire.

It has been said by one writer on ministerial life that the "most exasperating" missives in the "mass of annoying mail" a minister gets are questionnaires. In addition to assuming a right to intrude on his privacy, a questionnaire demands that the minister spend a good deal of time searching his memory and summoning his knowledge to find answers of value. It is safe to estimate that more than two-thirds of all questionnaires sent are ignored. Fortunately, this dire prediction did not hold true for our questionnaire. Of almost two thousand sent out, some eight hundred and seventy were returned with *all questions answered*—and answered with obvious care and interest.

An analysis of the answers received shows that the average age of the respondents was 70.2 years. The youngest was sixty-five; the oldest seventy-nine.

The average number of years in retirement was five years, one month. The shortest period of retirement was three years; the longest, thirteen years and seven months.

Here, question by question, is a summary of the replies:

*Question: Although a man may retire from a pastorate, he can hardly retire from the ministry. Pulpit supply, counseling, personal evangelism, group leadership, and civic responsibilities are among the wide variety of calls made upon him. What aspects of the ministry do you consider most important for a man to prepare to continue after retirement?*

Most of the respondents agreed on four major aspects: (1) pulpit supply; (2) counseling; (3) personal evangelism; and (4) theological study and research.

Said one man, speaking of pulpit supply: "I have been in retirement for four years, but in all this time I have had only fifteen Sundays free." Another commented: "There are so many avenues of faithful pastoral work open to ministers in retirement that I have had some of the richest and most satisfying experiences of my life since my official retirement."

*Question: Do you believe that ministers prepare adequately for retirement?*

The answer was unanimously "no." Ironically, in many cases the respondents added a statement to the effect that "this is probably my own experience only; undoubtedly most other ministers did a better job of preparing for their retirement."

*Question: What would you do differently if you were able to plan for your retirement again?*

Although the answers to this question were varied, by far the greatest emphasis was placed on better planning for financial security. Some typical comments were:

"I'd get a retirement insurance policy of some sort."

"I would make it an unbreakable rule to save a regular amount of money each week from the day of my acceptance of my first pastoral charge."

"I would make sure I had as adequate a pension plan as possible."

Next to financial security, the most stress was put on planning for post-retirement interests—avocations and hobbies.

One man said: "I'd make an earlier application for a place in a good home for the aged."

*Question: Have you moved to a different community from the one in which you served your last pastorate?*

Seventy per cent of the respondents said they had moved to a different community. Reasons (asked for in a follow-up question) varied widely. Here are some of them:

"I moved to the town that was my wife's former home."

"I moved so I could share an apartment with my daughter."

"I went to the city where I spent my young manhood because of the memories it held for me."

"I moved to a city that was the center of our denominational strength so that I could be more easily reached for pulpit supply work."

"I moved to my home town to be near old friends."

"I moved to a neighborhood across the city from the area of my old church, so that I wouldn't interfere with the activities of the new minister."

Apparent in the bulk of the replies to this question was one surprising fact: only a few retired ministers had chosen their new "home town" in a *positive* way: because, for example, it was an area where they could serve themselves or the community with new endeavors; or because it was a more healthful location, or somewhat more comfortable for retirement living. Here is one further bit of evidence of the general lack of retirement planning!

*Question: What do you consider is the biggest single problem facing the minister on retirement?*

Sixty per cent of the answers said that "getting enough

money to live without financial worries" was the biggest single problem to be faced. Thirty per cent emphasized the need to occupy the sudden abundance of leisure time. The remaining replies were divided among such difficulties as poor health, lack of friends, and feelings of uselessness with no calls for service.

*Question: If finances is the answer, what suggestions do you have for the minister to supplement his income?*

Neither imagination nor enterprise were reflected in the bulk of the answers to this question. The single suggestion mentioned more frequently than any other was, of course, pulpit supply. Beyond this, the answers often trailed off into seemingly half-hearted references to Social Security, suggestions on getting lecturing engagements, making "wise investments" during one's years of earning, raising rabbits and chickens. One man said simply: "Save more than is possible."

As you will see later in this book, however, there are literally scores of ways in which an alert retired minister can turn his talents—either ministerial or secular—to a variety of income-producing activities.

*Question: What is your annual income?*

Replies varied widely here, since income was reported from many diverse sources. The chief sources, however, were church pensions, insurance payments, and extra income from the pulpit supply or other work. (Of course, ministers who retire in and after 1956 will be able to include fairly solid Social Security payments in their income statements, and thereby can raise their total income considerably.)

For our respondents, however, the picture was far from rosy. Pension payments per year ran from a low of $300 to a high of $2,900. The average for all respondents was $1,484.

Insurance payments were surprisingly absent as a source of income. Most retired ministers seemed to have no insurance at all, or else owned small life policies which they had not converted or could not convert to *living* insurance—in other words, to a source of funds during their lifetime. (As we shall see later, wise counsel from an insurance expert when you are planning your insurance program can enable you to arrange your policies so that you yourself will get financial benefits from them in your later years.)

Annual earnings from pulpit supply and other activities ranged from a low of $140—to a high of $2,100. The average was $563 a year.

Adding the average income from pensions, insurance payments, earnings, we arrived at a total *average annual income* for our respondents of $2,047, or $39.36 a week.

With an income of two thousand dollars a year, our "average retired minister" does not have much of a Federal income tax problem. With double exemptions for himself and his wife (if they are both over sixty-five years of age)—he receives a total exemption under current law of $2,400. Thus he has no Federal tax at all to pay.

*Question: How do you spend your time?*

As you might imagine, this question drew a host of different replies. Encouragingly, virtually none of the respondents said they "did not know what to do," or had "nothing to do." On the one hand were many who specified "reading," "gardening," "walking in the country," or "caring for the house." On the other hand were many who seemed as much on the go as ever. "I am busy every minute," wrote one man. "I rise at 5:45 a.m. every day, and retire at 10 p.m. My day is scheduled. I have several things going, and work by the clock."

Another wrote: "I am a part-time chaplain for Goodwill Industries, secretary of the committee of chaplains of my church, and have been made president of the board of national missions."

Others mentioned pulpit supply work in small churches;

writing of sermons; personal counseling; civic and community activities; and teaching Bible classes.

*Question: What community activities do you think a minister can or should participate in?*

As might be expected, the answers emphasized such church activities as counseling, serving as chaplain to civic and community groups, and so on. Many reported active work with charitable drives; a few said they were concentrating their interests on children's and youth activities. Others worked with groups of older persons. Said one retired minister, with confident aggressiveness: "All community work that time and strength will permit!"

*Question: If you could tell other ministers how to prepare for retirement now, what would be your advice?*

Retired ministers were anxious to give suggestions to their brethren facing the same problems. Here are some representative comments:

"Get acquainted early with a hobby which will really intrigue and interest you."

"Arrange for a pension and retirement insurance. Too many younger ministers neglect to do the former unless it is compulsory; and younger ministers evidently do not think wisely about their future, when their insurance payments would be lowest."

"Make contacts in the community where you expect to spend your retirement years."

"Save, save, save."

"Have firm faith that God will get you something to do."

And—perhaps the best advice of all: "Never let worry about the future spoil the present for you."

*Question: If you could tell them the most important things they might do when retired—for their happiness, the good of the community, or what have you—what would your suggestions be?*

Service and religious faith were the keynotes of the responses to this last query on the questionnaire.

"Keeping busy" was emphasized by most of the retired ministers. Said one: "Keep your mind employed, keep regular hours, engage in social activities and recreational projects."

"Be ready to help" was the second theme of the answers. "Don't lose touch with your community or your church," wrote one man. "Carry on 'in character' as a minister of the Gospel of Christ."

Now let us go on to the problems at hand. Let us survey—step by step and chapter by chapter—the ways in which you can guide yourself to a successful retirement.

*Chapter Three*

# YOUR PERSONAL FINANCES

"No sane man ever enters the ministry with the thought of making money. He knows that he is enlisting in a service that will require thrift and self-denial as long as he lives.

"But there are limits to the sacrifices which the church has a right to ask . . . A man who embarks upon the ministry as a calling should feel assured that his days, and those of his wife, will be ended in decent comfort and with full self-respect.

"The churches want as leaders men with intelligence enough to be aware of the future, and with foresight enough to insist that it be secure."

These penetrating words are the observations of Dr. Frank Scribner, writing about pension plans in the March, 1949, issue of *The Missionary Herald.* What he had to say then is still true. It is in fact even more cogent and significant today, for our nation waxes ever richer and healthier. Our standard of living spirals higher and higher. Families which in the not-too-distant past could barely afford one rattling, patched-together, second-hand car are now two-car families; television antennas reach skyward in every part of town, rich and poor. Nevertheless our older citizens, and our citizens in traditionally low-paid fields, find that this era of prosperity is somehow a time when it is still difficult to make ends meet. And the battle is grimmest for the retired minister!

We know that he has not been able to put money away for a rainy day—or for the potentially-bright day of retirement. We know that he has not been able to make the kind of investments which yield considerable returns in his later years. We know from surveys and familiar case-histories that he rarely is covered by the right kind and quantity of insurance; and when he does have a policy, it is not often enough the sort which can be converted to tidy, regular annuity payments.

And then there's the matter of housing. Census figures show that in the United States roughly half of the couples over the age of sixty-five own their own homes; indeed, a major financial goal during their earlier years was the amortization of the mortgages on their homes. But when the minister reaches sixty-five and retirement—he takes on, possibly for the first time in his life, the considerable burdens of rent or mortgage payments. During his church service he lived rent-free at a parsonage or rectory; or he received part of his salary specifically *for* rent. Now he has a substantially decreased income—and monthly rent bills!

Rare is the minister who is able to apply part of his salary to buying a home and furnishing it. I think of one friend who is pastor of an important church in a large New England community. His rectory was willed to the church by a wealthy family in the congregation; it is a vast, sprawling house—twenty rooms on the first two floors, and the third floor is a huge, Victorian-era ballroom. To heat the house alone costs two thousand dollars a year. Old-fashioned fixtures made good lighting impossible. To keep it running, the minister's wife has become a one-woman task force: her day is an eternity of cleaning, dusting, and scouring. How much better off they would be were that imposing rectory to tumble to the ground! How much better off if they could live in a small and cozy house, just big enough for their family of four! But instead, the congregation continues the delusion of a "rent-free home"—while every spare cent of the minister's income goes into making the "mansion" barely livable!

When he leaves it, what will he be able to take with him? Money enough to buy his own home? Furnishings? No, nothing but weariness!

Finally, the pressure of work during his active career does not permit the average minister to take on the kind of part-time jobs which can later be converted into income-producing skills. We all know ministers who add to their incomes with such menial and difficult chores as wrapping, packaging and shipping; we all have read of ministers who work as truck-drivers in order, literally, to feed and clothe and educate their children. But these are not jobs one could or would want to hold after retirement; the heart and body would not allow it.

And yet—the minister is often told that the key to the personal economics of his retirement is "advance planning and saving." No wonder that the usual response is this almost-frantic question: *"How?"*

We're about to *see* "how." But first, let us study a few statistics.

For example, figures developed during the 1950 census show that thirty per cent of American families in the sixty-five-and-older age group had incomes of under $1,000.00 a year. Twenty-one per cent received between $1,000.00 and $2,000.00 a year; sixteen per cent between $2,000.00 and $3,000.00; eighteen per cent between $3,000.00 and $5,000.00; and fifteen per cent over $5,000.00 a year. In other words, over half the families (and this means *couples* in the overwhelming number of cases) had annual incomes of less than $2,000.00 a year. Indeed, the *average* annual income was $986.00 a year—less than one thousand dollars.

Do these seem like impossibly low amounts on which to live in this day of high rent and food costs? If so, you will be surprised to learn that the President's Council of Economic Advisors has recently declared that $2,000.00 a year is *adequate* for an elderly couple. Here's why:

(1) You can cut your living expenses. With more time to call your own, you'll find yourself doing more of your own repairs and maintenance; perhaps you will grow a larger proportion of your own food; your wife will have time to can and preserve. Clothing can be more informal. If you move to a new locality, especially one in the South—where living costs in general are cheaper—you may find yourself able to effect cuts in expenses in all major categories.

(2) Expenses normally incurred by your work will drop off. Charitable contributions can now be more in line with your finances than, as formerly, with your position. Your expenses for professional trips, book clubs and magazines will lessen. You will eat more meals at home, fewer out.

(3) It is unlikely that other persons will still be dependent on you for financial support or aid. Children will have grown up and gone off on their own; older relatives will have passed on.

(4) Your taxes will be considerably lower, perhaps even non-existent. If a man and wife are both over sixty-five, the combined total of their personal exemption is (at this writing) $2,400, without even starting to count such other deductible expenses as medical care, charitable contributions, local taxes, and so on. Social Security benefits are tax-free, and pension and annuity income is taxed on such a basis (as you will see in a forthcoming chapter) as to make it a very minor item.

(5) The big "bulk" expenditures will no longer arise. You will no longer have to meet heavy college tuition fees for the youngsters; and your insurance premium payments will probably be considerably lower, or non-existent.

In other words, you will be able to maintain approximately the same standard of living you've been used to—but on less money.

The key phrase, of course, is "standard of living." The unfortunate older persons are those who have a "champagne and caviar" taste and a "bread and potatoes" budget. But because the average minister has never lived (or even wanted) a "champagne and caviar" kind of existence, he will find the transition a good deal easier.

One of the first steps you should take in facing up to the financial realities of retirement is to get down in black and white just what your income-and-expense situation will be. In other words, set up a budget. Make it a flexible one, and view it as a friendly guide rather than as a compelling leader. It should function as a compass—pointing the direction in which you are heading, financially, but not strictly and sternly limiting your way of life. Basically, a budget serves best when it gives you a graphic picture of what is happening; and often such insight alone is sufficient to keep you on an even financial keel.

Your personal budget need not be complicated. On one side, list your monthly income. Normally this will consist of income from investments, life insurance policies, pension fund payments, and Social Security benefits.

Then estimate your monthly expenses. The broad general headings for these are usually rent, heating, utilities, food, clothing, medical expenses, entertainment, and personal expenses—hair cuts, for example, and tobacco and carfare.

If your income is greater than your expenses, you can plan to "loosen up" in one or another of the categories;

or, better yet, you can plan to put the extra money aside for emergency needs.

If the expenses are equal with or larger than the income, you will then search out areas in which to cut costs; or you will want to give some thought to ways of earning extra money from part-time work (see Chapters Six and Seven).

None of this advice is new or startling. But you'll be surprised to see how much firmer a grasp you'll have of your financial position, and the steps you need to take about it, once you have your overall situation clearly pictured.

If, for example, your expenses are outrunning your income and nothing can be done about it, you will know the extent to which you are dipping into savings. And you will have advance warning when the backlog begins to wear thin.

Do you feel that it's impossible to judge today what your living expenses are likely to be tomorrow? Surprisingly enough, *percentages* change very little over the years. The government recently prepared an "average annual budget" for elderly couples; it was based on average prices in the year 1950, and it's worth your careful examination. It can be a valuable guide to your retirement planning.

The "budget family"—let's call them Mr. and Mrs. Brown—are assumed to be a husband and wife of about sixty-five years of age. They rent an apartment (or "flat" or the wing of a home) which consists of three rooms. The dwelling is unfurnished: it has a sink and a stove, hot and cold running water, a private bathroom with tub or shower; electricity; and some form of heating. In addition, the location of the home is not more than ten blocks from a bus, trolley, railroad, elevated or subway line; and the dwelling is safe and sanitary.

Mr. Brown is retired from full-time work. Mrs. Brown is not employed. They have no car. Their budget is based on a standard of living described by the Bureau of Labor

Statistics as "modest but adequate." It includes all items "necessary for a healthful, self-respecting mode of living which allows normal participation in the life of the community in accordance with current American standards."

Depending on where they decided to live, the Browns could get along for as little as $1,602.00 a year in New Orleans, Louisiana—or, at the same standard of living, for a high of $1,908.00 a year in Milwaukee, Wisconsin. Housing makes the big difference; in New Orleans, for example, it costs $436.00 a year, while in Milwaukee the very same kind of dwelling would rent for $705 a year.

Other living expenses, however, show little variation from community to community. Food, clothing, the cost of house furnishings, medical and personal care, transportation, home maintenance, and recreation—the total sum for all these products and services for Mr. and Mrs. Brown range from a low of $1,126.00 a year in Savannah, Georgia, to $1,269.00 a year in Seattle, Washington. Here is where America's emphasis on "name brand" products, price-fixed merchandise and standardized operations has most effect: a difference of only twelve dollars a month in non-housing living costs between the "least expensive" and one of the seven "most expensive" cities in the country!

You'll note that six of the ten "least expensive" cities in the table below are Southern cities. Low-cost housing is one reason; and the opportunity to raise poultry and grow vegetables on a year-round basis is another. Obviously, other factors contribute to the fact that it's easier to get along on less in the South: one's winter-clothing needs are substantially reduced, for example.

Yet it would be dangerous to assume from these figures that one could move, let us say, to Mobile, Alabama, and expect to thrive on precisely $1,620.00 a year. Remember that these are October, 1950, statistics; because living costs have risen substantially since then it would be proper to

*Dollar costs of elderly couple's total budget, housing, and other goods and services, 34 cities—October 1950*

DOLLAR COSTS

| CITY AND STATE | TOTAL BUDGET | HOUSING | OTHER GOODS AND SERVICES |
|---|---|---|---|
| New Orleans, La. | $1,602 | $436 | $1,166 |
| Scranton, Pa. | 1,614 | 463 | 1,151 |
| Mobile, Ala. | 1,620 | 475 | 1,145 |
| Cincinnati, Ohio | 1,650 | 485 | 1,165 |
| Savannah, Ga. | 1,658 | 532 | 1,126 |
| Kansas City, Mo. | 1,687 | 507 | 1,180 |
| Buffalo, N.Y. | 1,698 | 534 | 1,164 |
| St. Louis, Mo. | 1,711 | 527 | 1,184 |
| Richmond, Va. | 1,712 | 581 | 1,131 |
| Memphis, Tenn. | 1,726 | 563 | 1,163 |
| Portland, Maine | 1,733 | 548 | 1,185 |
| Manchester, N.H. | 1,737 | 550 | 1,187 |
| Indianapolis, Ind. | 1,746 | 569 | 1,177 |
| Denver, Colo. | 1,746 | 577 | 1,169 |
| Atlanta, Ga. | 1,748 | 582 | 1,166 |
| Minneapolis, Minn. | 1,765 | 577 | 1,188 |
| Pittsburgh, Pa. | 1,767 | 554 | 1,213 |
| Birmingham, Ala. | 1,772 | 607 | 1,165 |
| Norfolk, Va. | 1,774 | 612 | 1,162 |
| Baltimore, Md. | 1,779 | 603 | 1,176 |
| New York, N.Y. | 1,782 | 543 | 1,239 |
| Philadelphia, Pa. | 1,783 | 587 | 1,196 |
| Jacksonville, Fla. | 1,795 | 621 | 1,174 |
| Cleveland, Ohio | 1,805 | 590 | 1,215 |
| Chicago, Ill. | 1,818 | 578 | 1,240 |
| Detroit, Mich. | 1,818 | 573 | 1,245 |
| San Francisco, Calif. | 1,833 | 567 | 1,266 |
| Seattle, Wash. | 1,852 | 583 | 1,269 |
| Houston, Tex. | 1,855 | 670 | 1,185 |
| Washington, D.C. | 1,863 | 671 | 1,192 |
| Los Angeles, Calif. | 1,866 | 605 | 1,261 |
| Portland, Ore. | 1,866 | 630 | 1,236 |
| Boston, Mass. | 1,880 | 640 | 1,240 |
| Milwaukee, Wis. | 1,908 | 705 | 1,203 |

add about $150 to each figure to approximate current costs. On the other hand, two important insights *may* be gained from the chart: first—you'll need less money than you think. And second—you'll be better off if you choose your place of abode on the basis of facts, not happenstance or wishful thinking.

A minimum target for ministers, then, would be the assurance of an income of no less than two thousand dollars a year after retirement.

*And that's precisely the sum—$2,047.00—found to be the "average annual income" of the ministers who responded in the survey conducted by the author and publishers of this book!*

But our aim should and must go higher than this "minimum target." An income so tight and so carefully-budgeted that one cannot make an impulse purchase—a book, a gift for one's wife, or a new suit—is scarcely a fitting goal for a man who has served his life in a field requiring "thrift and self-denial" to an abnormal degree. Thus you'll find that the emphasis in this book is on your two best ways to obtain the income which gives one the margin to buy what economic experts call the "necessary luxuries of life." The first method: insurance and pension planning. The second, part-time earning opportunities.

Where do *most* retired couples get the money on which they live? From a variety of sources—accumulated savings, insurance annuities, interest from investments, the sale of businesses, the sale of stocks and bonds accumulated over the years, pensions, and Social Security payments.

Where do ministers get the money on which to live?

Not usually from accumulated savings, since their profession is not one which normally allows regular putting-aside of capital.

Not from the sale of businesses; nor from selling and trading accumulated stocks and bonds.

Not often enough from annuities, as we have seen, although this can be perhaps the cheapest and safest way to build a margin of comfort into your retirement life. Some ministers apparently believe they can ignore the question of insurance coverage until the morning of their retirement; that they at this point can purchase the kind of protection that will bring them a steady $100 or $200 a month for the rest of their lives. It can be done—but at a cost high in the five-figure bracket! Were such a plan launched at age thirty or forty, on the other hand, payments would be relatively modest in return for the security offered at sixty or sixty-five. This subject will be treated thoroughly in a later chapter of the book; suffice it to say for now that annuity income is unfortunately missing in the financial pictures of too many ministers.

Nor can ministers expect to get their retirement income from investments. Under the present tax laws, it would require an annual income of something like *fifty thousand dollars a year* to enable a man to invest sufficient funds in bonds or conservative stocks to get a retirement income in interest payments of about *one hundred dollars a month!*

Thus—the average minister must look to pension plans for the *core* of his retirement income. Our survey showed that the average sum received under such plans was $1,484.00 a year; and that the highest was less than three thousand dollars annually. These are not princely sums . . . yet when you begin with a pension plan producing up to about thirty dollars a week, and add to it Social Security payments of another thirty to forty dollars weekly, you arrive at a sum which is at least over the "minimum target" for adequate living.

This book cannot tell you the details of the denominational pension plan in which you as an individual may participate. They vary too considerably to allow coverage in the limited space of one volume. All we can do is urge

the entire question of church-state relationship; otherwise the question of the federal government's right to tax religious bodies would arise. For another, it makes it possible for a minister to get Social Security coverage without the agreement of his church.

Unlike most other self-employed persons—who MUST pay Social Security taxes—ministers have the right to accept or refuse this coverage. Thus any man with religious or political scruples against Social Security is free to go along without it, while at the same time not denying its benefits to others.

Since coverage is voluntary, a minister must do something about getting himself enrolled. Here are the steps you should take, and the facts you should know, to be certain you are not now losing or will not in the future lose any Social Security benefits.

*Eligibility:* To be eligible, a minister must earn at least $400 a year "in the exercise of his ministry." This phrase has been interpreted as including not only his church-paid salary, but also fees received for the performance of such ceremonies as weddings, funerals, and baptisms. "Income received in the exercise of the ministry" even includes free-will offerings taken up at meetings. The $400 minimum sum to be earned is the only major requirement; *it does not make any difference how old you are on January 1, 1955.*

*Next Steps:* To qualify for benefits a minister must do three things:

*1.* Get a Social Security card and account number. You can apply for these either in person or by mail at the nearest Social Security Administration Field Office. Any post office can tell you where your area Field Office is located; or you can find it listed in the telephone directory under the heading, "U.S. Government, Department of Health, Education and Welfare." In smaller towns the Field Office is often in the same federal building which houses the post office.

*2.* Fill out a standard, printed form on which you

declare your desire to be covered by Social Security. These forms are provided by local Internal Revenue (income tax) Bureaus, but are also usually available at any Social Security field office, and sometimes even at your neighborhood post office.

*3.* Pay your Social Security taxes. This is done at the same time that you pay the last installment of your Federal income tax. You will see that a special schedule is included with the tax form to cover the Social Security payments of self-employed persons; note too that if a minister is covered by Social Security as of January 1, 1955, his Social Security tax for that year won't be payable until the spring of 1956. The tax is added to and made a part of his income tax payment; at the present time, the *most* anyone can pay in such taxes in one year is $126.00.

It's the better part of wisdom to go on record *as promptly as possible* as wanting Social Security coverage. You can procrastinate for a while, we admit: in order to obtain coverage as of January 1, 1955, you need not file the certificate described in Point Two above until the Spring of 1956. But there is always a danger in putting things off—the danger of forgetting, of making an error which delays the routine considerably. And even more important: because of the peculiar earning requirements we'll discuss later in this chapter, it's particularly urgent that the older minister make absolutely sure that he gets under Social Security coverage *at once.*

*Benefits:* Before you can actually receive Social Security payments, you must be at least sixty-five years old; and you must be "fully insured." Under Social Security definition of that phrase, a man must have been under Social Security coverage for a minimum of six quarterly periods—in other words, eighteen months. Further, he must either:

*1.* have paid Social Security taxes upon income for forty "quarter-years" (ten years); *or,*

2. have paid Social Security taxes upon income for *half* the quarter-years starting with January, 1951, and ending the year before he reaches age sixty-five; *or,*

3. have paid Social Security taxes upon income for all the quarter-years between January 1, 1955, and July 1, 1956 (or the quarter in which a man reaches age sixty-five, or dies).

Since virtually everyone can qualify for coverage under one or another of these regulations, the next question is—how much do you get? And do the number and cash amount of payments have any relation to the length of coverage?

Answering the second question first; they do not. A fully insured man gets the same benefits—in proportion to his average earnings—whether he has been covered for the minimum year-and-a-half or whether he has been paying Social Security taxes for forty years. (Yet the plan does not deprive the younger man: he will eventually receive as much—if not more—than the total amount he has paid in.)

As to the size of the benefit payments themselves: they are approximately equal to 55% of the first $110 of the minister's average monthly wage.

You'll note that payments are based upon the fixed standard of the "average monthly wage"; with a little paper-and-pencil work you can figure out exactly what your benefits will be in dollars and cents.

Here is an example: Minister Jones will be sixty-five years old in 1960, and he earns $5,000 a year. Since the maximum salary on which Social Security taxes may be paid is $4,200 a year, we disregard the remaining $800 of Minister Jones' income.

To estimate his benefits, Jones lists the years, beginning with 1951 and ending with the year before his benefit payments begin. (He uses the second of the three definitions of being "fully insured," listed a few lines previously.) Opposite each year he writes the amount of earnings on which he paid Social Security taxes; NOT, we emphasize, his total earnings if they exceed or at any time did exceed $4,200.

| | |
|---|---|
| 1951—$0 | 1955—$4,200 |
| 1952— 0 | 1956— 4,200 |
| 1953— 0 | 1957— 4,200 |
| 1954— 0 | 1958— 4,200 |
| 1959— 4,200 | |

He adds this column and gets a total of $21,000. Then he deducts from this sum the amount he received for four years during which he paid the smallest amount of Social Security taxes. In a minister's case, of course (since he was not eligible until 1955), those years will be 1951-55, and the sum will be zero. So we are still left with $21,000.

Then Minister Jones starts counting up the months; he counts the months from January, 1951, to the end of the year before which his benefits start. Twelve months a year for the nine years from 1951 through 1959 equal 108 months. From this he subtracts the forty-eight months during which his Social Security-taxed income was zero. The remaining figure—sixty months—he divides into the $21,000 sum. The answer—$350—is Jones' "average monthly wage."

Taking 55% of the first $110 of this yields $60.50; 20% of the remaining $240 yields $48.00. Adding them up we get $108.50—the amount of Social Security benefit Jones will receive every month for the rest of his life.

Better yet, once Jones' wife reaches sixty-five, *she* gets an additional amount equal to one-half of his basic payment. That would be $54.25, making a *total monthly benefit* to the Joneses of $162.75. If Jones dies after he has started to draw Social Security payments, his surviving wife will continue to get one-half of this latter amount—or $81.38—as long as she lives.

This is a fair bit of income, especially if it can be combined with life insurance annuity payments, a church pension, or similar other incomes.

*Costs and Restrictions:* What does it cost you to qualify

for it? And what restrictions are placed on you if you receive payments?

First, the cost is minor. It can be so only because millions of American workers and employers are contributing to the build-up of Social Security funds, while at the present time only a small proportion of the population is drawing benefits. An employed person shares the cost of Social Security with his employer, both of whom pay an equal percentage of a man's salary into the fund. But a self-employed person pays less than this combined amount (although he *does* pay slightly more than the employed man alone).

At present, the tax is 3% per year on *the first $4,200 only* of income, or a maximum of $126. Any income above that amount is excluded from consideration for Social Security purposes. In 1960, this tax percentage will rise to 3¾% of the first $4,200 of income. Every five years thereafter it will go up another three quarters of one per cent until 1975, when it reaches its maximum of 6%.

This amount must be paid by the minister himself, not by his church or congregation—although there are obvious ways of their reimbursing him for it, if desired.

Remember that income includes a minister's salary less expenses incurred in earning it; it includes any fees he may receive for officiating at ceremonies; but it does not include rental value of a church-supplied parsonage, or any expense allowance.

Now for the restrictions: if you are between the ages of sixty-five and seventy-two and getting Social Security benefits, any monies over $1,200 a year that you earn must be deducted from your benefits. (Money from gifts or pension plans or retirement funds are not included in this restriction —only *earned* income.) But once you are past seventy-two years of age, you can earn any amount at all without its having any effect on your Social Security payments. This ruling is a recent relaxation of Social Security restrictions; future public pressure may relax them even more.

Although I have tried to keep this explanation as simple as possible, the Social Security laws are an extraordinarily complex set of legislation. Any summary of its basic regulations must incorporate various generalizations; there are bound to be exceptions in many individual cases.

It would be wise in any event, then, to discuss the application of the Social Security law to your own position with either a field representative of the local Social Security Administration (they are most helpful), or with your own attorney or accountant.

For example, a man who is now sixty-three years and six months old has a special problem: the average monthly wage formula, on which the amount of his benefit payments depends, is based on full-year figures. So although this man will be technically "fully insured" with his eighteen months coverage, his "average wage" figures will be quite low. But if he worked another six months and had *two* full years' coverage, his average wage calculation—and his benefits—would zoom up.

There are many similar exceptions, conditions and qualifications that can pay off in extra benefits for many years if you know about them, and make proper use of them.

But what about the already-retired minister who is excluded from Social Security coverage? Some congregations and churches are finding ways to make it possible for these men to earn at least $400 a year during two consecutive years—and thus to qualify for Social Security benefits.

These churches are either employing their retired pastors in some kind of limited service; or are making sure they are called upon for paid advisory work; or are hiring them in pulpit supply work.

If you have already retired and are without Social Security benefits, it would be wise for you to discuss this situation and these possibilities with your present minister at once.

*Chapter Five*

# YOUR INSURANCE PROGRAM

World War II wrought a revolutionary change in American concepts; for the first time, the people of this nation came to feel that tomorrow's security is as important as today's challenging opportunity. Look, if you will, at the "Help Wanted" section of any newspaper; the advertisements you find there do not feature the promise that one can "work his way up from office-boy to vice-president." They do not stress that "hard work means rapid advancement." No—American employers now talk in terms of pensions, seniority, hospitalization, sickness insurance, guaranteed annual wages, retirement funds, profit-sharing, low-cost company loans, group life insurance, and so on through the ever-increasing catalogue of "fringe benefits" designed to create a secure future.

We've become a nation of people who say: "I know I can handle the problems of today. It's the uncertainty of tomorrow that I must guard against." Thus we no longer simply save for a rainy day; we go farther, and attempt to build our own individual Arks of financial protection.

This change of philosophy is perhaps most evident in the field of insurance. Putting the facts in their most succinct form: It's no longer necessary for you to die to make your insurance policy worthwhile! America's insurance companies now prefer that you buy *living* insurance; and to that end, they have revised their planning and actuarial statistics, devised new policies, and broadened their operations immeasurably. The result is that today rates are lower and protection greater, with ever more Americans covered than at any time in history.

If this book were written for engineers, let us say, or advertising executives, no further discussion of insurance would be needed. It would suffice to say that an insurance program is recommended; that it would be a useful supplement to large-company "fringe benefits"; that it is not inexpensive; but that on the other hand, nothing is more expensive than *not* having insurance when it is sorely needed.

Yes, for lawyers or advertising executives or factory-workers, this advice would be sufficient. Not for the minister, however; his income potential, his kind of work, his lack of most "fringe benefits," and even his life expectancy make the question a different one. Again and again the minister must be made to realize that his retirement problems demand an intelligent protection program, supplementing his Social Security and denominational plans. The clergyman should have started to do something about insurance the day he entered his seminary; and he should continue to do something about it all his working life.

This being the case, it is fortunate that you—the American minister—are a "preferred risk." Your work and your living habits promise an unusually long life expectancy.

Ministers do not shorten their lives with the abuses of liquor and "high living"; they do not strain their hearts with a competitive, driving struggle for the outward show of success; they do not puff away nervously at three packs of cigarettes a day, and then dope themselves into slumber at night with sleeping pills. One does not read of ministers careening down the highways in cars that screech along at eighty miles an hour. The minister has achieved a calm center for his life.

Thus, the life expectancy of the average young clergyman is about five and a half years greater than that of the average male. As Louis I. Dublin and Mortimer Spiegelman declare in their brilliant and authoritative book, *Length of Life* (Ronald Press, New York):

"In the peace and security of . . . an American parsonage, the minister at the beginning of his professional career may look forward to a ripe old age. His chances of enjoying a long and healthy life are greater than if he had chosen almost any other occupation."

Yes, in every sense of the word, you are in a preferred category.

Even with this advantageous situation, however—is it financially possible for you to purchase a policy that will protect your retirement years? Let's examine a typical example:

Minister Jones is now forty years old, active, and in average good health. He serves in a denomination which makes retirement at sixty-five mandatory; his wife and he, therefore, look forward to a retirement highlighted by travel and occasional fishing trips.

Jones has prepared—as suggested in an earlier chapter—an anticipated retirement budget. He has reckoned his likely income from his pension fund and Social Security payments. And he finds that an additional fifty dollars a month income would make complete retirement possible; any earnings over that sum would allow more of the "little luxuries" of life.

There are two ways in which he can assure himself of this $600.00 a year of added income. He can now begin a careful, intensive campaign to save a specific amount of money each week. But Minister Jones spots two immediate flaws in this plan: first, far too few of us actually live up to such good intentions—we let one week go by, then another, and ultimately our firm resolve and worthy goals wither away and die. Second, and far more important—Jones knows that money in a savings-bank offers no extra protection to his wife and children if he dies. But that same money, invested in an endowment insurance policy, offers protection which is always far above the cash investment.

And so Jones decides to investigate a retirement insurance program designed to bring him an assured fifty dollars a month, every month for the rest of his life, beginning at age sixty-five. He does this knowing full well that he is admittedly investigating the most expensive form of insurance currently sold.

And it *is* relatively expensive. Depending on the various benefits of particular policies, and the particular companies writing them, it will cost somewhere between $263.80 and $285.00 a year for the next twenty-five years. About seventy-five to seventy-nine cents a day if paid on a quarterly basis.

But with pencil and paper, Jones figures out what he will receive for this yearly payment. The list of benefits is impressive indeed!

His policy will have a guaranteed maturity value of more than $8,000.00 when it is completely paid up. In other words, Jones' money has been at work all these years, producing interest which totals to at least $1,500.00 and very likely somewhat more.

Jones knows that the same sums deposited in a savings-bank would produce even greater profit; yet he also realizes that were he to die even a week after signing this retirement-income policy, his wife would collect the full face value of his policy. In this case, his beneficiary would be given a check for $5,000.00. No ordinary savings plan can promise this sort of protection.

Let's not forget, however, that this is not Jones' primary aim in his insurance plan; were he merely seeking protection for his family, he could obtain far more for far less were he simply to buy straight term insurance.

No—it's that guaranteed income of $50.00 a month that

Jones is seeking to assure. And that's what this plan delivers. Even then, however, it does not lose its family-protection aspects: for if Jones were to die before he reached seventy-five, his beneficiary would receive regular monthly payments for the balance of the period.

With all things considered, then—his costs, current dividend rates, and maturity value—Minister Jones can anticipate a *profit* of approximately $3,000.00 on his protection program.

This author has had the grim experience of reading report after report from retired ministers; again and again they describe the vicious struggle necessary to scrape up dimes and dollars for the costs of later-year living. This experience alone makes him urge every reader to look life squarely in the face—and move ahead quickly toward insurance protection.

But what if you cannot afford a retirement policy? Does this mean that you should give up all thought of insurance security?

Scarcely—quite the reverse is indicated! You should then investigate other policies.

The law of averages is kind to ministers on the one hand; but on the other, the fact is that before reaching age seventy, four ministers out of every ten will be disabled by sickness or accident for more than three months; one in nine will be invalided for more than a year. Sieges of such seriousness and duration can wipe out a retirement nest-egg with startling speed; and so the cautious minister may well consider an inexpensive disability insurance plan. Quarterly costs for a man forty-five years of age or less—producing monthly benefits of $150.00 for as long as ten years—can be purchased for as little as about ten dollars a month.

This leads us to a point I want to emphasize: *do not purchase a major policy without a "waiver of premium" clause*!

This will normally be available in all Life policies except for certain term insurance agreements.

What *is* "waiver of premium"? It's an exceedingly low-cost addition to your program which guarantees that your full protection will continue even if total disability makes it impossible for you to meet premium payments. Just as statistics show that a large number of ministers will be disabled by sickness or accident before they are seventy, so do they show that total disability comes to many men, preventing them from preserving the protection their family will now need more than ever. "Waiver of premium" benefits literally cost only pennies a day; no purchaser should fail to take advantage of them.

You must have gathered long before you reached this chapter—and you will certainly realize it all the more keenly as you read the following chapters on part-time earning opportunities, travel, and housing—that I prefer to show you how to save money, not spend it. Yet there is one more point I must make in this frank advice to you to spend for the security of insurance. And that is the question of your wife's future when you retire.

Your denominational pension plan and Social Security payments, as we have seen, can amount to a minimum adequate income; but upon your death, both of these are usually halved. The resulting sum is rarely adequate for comfortable, secure living.

Yet the chances are that your wife will survive you by as many as seven years. The life expectancy of a woman is some five years greater than that of a man of the same age; moreover, men usually marry women who are their juniors by two years or more. Thus, an inadequate protection program can mean long, difficult and painful years for your widow.

Let's sum it up this way: there is a program suitable to your needs if you merely look for it. If you're forty years old and cannot afford to spend $264.00 or $285.00 a year for one type of retirement protection, you'll be able to get something "almost as good" for less in an endowment-at-age-sixty-five plan. If that too is still too costly, you can consider an "adjusted protection" policy of one sort or another. Or you can take out a term policy which is convertible to Ordinary Life or Endowment within the insurance period.

Let the insurance company know your problems, your needs, and your ideas on what sort of protection will fit your individual case. In their files—out of their actual experience, working with many thousands of people—will come an answer to assure peace of mind when you leave your last ministry, and begin your good years of retirement.

*Chapter Six*

# HOW TO MAKE EXTRA MONEY

In a play that recently opened on Broadway, one line of dialogue stunned the audience with its cynical, startling reversal of the normal values of life.

"What good is happiness?" asked the heroine. "Can it buy money?"

Well, oddly enough there *is* at least one time in a man's life when the achievement of personal happiness actually does, in effect, buy money. That's when he selects a truly suitable and congenial post-retirement business activity.

No single thing contributes as much to a retired person's health and emotional happiness as his ability to continue to do useful and constructive work. And one by-product of such work, of course, is money.

In this phase of his retirement, the minister is more fortunate than most men. By virtue of his education, training, and experience, he is fitted for an unusual number of money-earning activities. To him are open not only the whole wide range of small-business activities, but the more cultural vineyards of teaching, lecturing, and writing as well. Moreover, the minister can logically seek full- or part-time employment in community or charitable ventures; in serving with youth groups or religious groups; and indeed, in any field in which a man of solidity, probity and wisdom would be an asset.

In this chapter we'll explore ways in which you can make extra money in the cultural fields. Opportunities for additional income from business ventures, mail-order operations and the like will be detailed in the following chapter. But let us begin with two words of caution: First, don't try to make money or find peace of mind doing something which represents a complete and sudden break from the things you have been doing all your life. If, for example, you've never seen a chicken except on a platter at the Sunday dinner table, it would probably be unwise for you to try to go into the business of raising chickens. And if you never wrote for publication before your retirement, the chances are you ought not attempt a post-retirement career in journalism or literature.

Second, you'll find that work opportunities vary considerably with the community in which you make your home. If you retire to a small town far from the highways of big-city civilization, you're likely to have a hard time getting pulpit supply work; and it may be equally difficult to find opportunities for lecturing or counseling. The opportunities will simply not be there. On the other hand, your small town may produce some little-known local product or arts-and-crafts handiwork which you can develop into a successful item for the mail-order business. Those retired Americans who sell decorative fish-netting to "city folks"—who ship Maine maple syrup to the other forty-seven states—who find an excellent mail-order market for ceramic pottery made in New Mexico—would scarcely have come upon these opportunities had they stayed, let us say, in Chicago. Generally, in fact, big-city competition for any kind of earning activity is more strenuous than in America's middle-population centers.

The moral, then, is this: Learn what you can do best; and choose the area in which you'll do it carefully!

### PULPIT SUPPLY

This is probably the first branch of post-retirement work considered by ministers. And naturally so, for it merges their abilities with the church's needs. But like anything else, being asked to supply pulpits is a matter of both luck and planning.

In a previous chapter ("How to Leave Your Congregation Gracefully"), all the quoted authorities recommended that the retiring minister remove himself from the scene of his former triumphs, thus leaving the field clear and open for his successor. But the plain fact is that there will be many more opportunities for you in pulpit supply work if you live, after retirement, in an area where you have friends in the ministry and the congregation.

It becomes your task, therefore, to find the best compromise between these two needs: being geographically available without seeming to be perched on the premises of your old church like Edgar Allen Poe's raven.

Although ministers are, by nature and training, modest men, the overly-shrinking violet will never get his fair share of pulpit supply work: people simply will not know he's available and interested. If you do want to be considered for fill-in preaching, you must make sure that the local minister *and* the congregation *and* the regional authorities of your church are aware of your availability. And you must avoid like the plague living in any area where there is a theological seminary!

It takes tact to do this properly. True, the job seldom goes to the man who chases after it; but it *never* goes to the man who no one knows is there.

"Pulpit supply work can be lots of fun," Dr. John Scotford told me. "To do a good job of it, however, a man must be a consummate politician, needs a wealth of experience in dealing with people of all kinds, and, above all, must know what to believe and what to discount in the flood of rumor and gossip with which he'll soon be deluged.

"The retired minister who is supplying a pulpit has nothing to gain or lose, and thus can handle a situation with a complete absence of strain or pressure. And he can also get away with more innovations because he is not setting any precedents."

On rare occasions, pulpit supply work can lead to astonishing results. One retired minister was called on to supply a pulpit when the regular minister suffered a physical collapse—a nervous breakdown brought on by long-standing arguments with various prominent members of his congregation. The interim minister did so fine a job of fence-mending and compromising difficulties during the six months of his service that at the end of his term the congregation chipped in and gave him a vacation trip to Europe.

But the average man receives no such glamorous reward for his fill-in job. He comes to his church; he serves the needs of the congregation as best he can; and leaves when the regular minister returns.

If this sounds like a thankless task, listen to the inspiring words of Walter Schuette about the work of pulpit supply:

"What an opportunity to show how experience in the Ministry can teach a man to reach people's hearts. What an opportunity to weave thoughts into the sermon which will heighten people's regard for their regular minister and increase the appreciation of what the minister endures and accomplishes! What an opportunity to display one's imperishable spiritual youth and one's practical up-to-datedness!"

There are other opportunities for church work apart from pulpit supply. Some retired ministers, for example, have made an interesting, profitable and highly useful career for themselves out of "patching up" quarreling congregations. A man with experience and a warm, outgoing personality—a man who brings a fresh and objective viewpoint to the scene of a conflict—can work wonders in smoothing the troubled waters that now and again bubble up. The Methodist Church, in particular, makes use of retired ministers for this purpose. And such work is immensely satisfying personally: it is truly constructive, and truly a tribute to one's abilities and personality.

Occasionally a large city church will find itself in need of trained clergymen who are willing to make personal calls on congregation members, doing religious and personal counseling under the general supervision of the permanent staff. It takes a certain amount of grace and tact for the church to offer a retired minister what might be considered a subordinate job; and it takes an equal amount of grace and tact for the man who has once been in complete charge of his own church to accept a less-than-leading role with another's flock. Yet here again, pride is best assuaged by the realization that an experienced minister's training can be invaluable in helping men and women find the strength and love of faith. And psychologically, you will find that all of these phases of post-retirement church work offer excellent ways of "tapering off," of easing the transition from full time work to full time retirement.

Perhaps some day a forward-looking group will do for retired ministers what the John Whitney Foundation recently did for retired professors. Under the Whitney Foundation's program, funds are made available so that retired teachers who have outstanding reputations in their fields are able to visit and teach for a semester or a year at small colleges, thus spreading their learning and philosophies among students who otherwise would not be able to benefit from them.

Why shouldn't a similar arrangement work to allow outstanding retiring ministers to be guest preachers for a period of time at small churches?

### LECTURING

For a vivid speaker, lecturing seems at first glance to be an excellent source of post-retirement income. But unless you have an exceptionally exciting and newsworthy subject—and a particularly forceful, personal and expressive manner of speaking—the lecture podium actually offers only dim prospects for a career.

Lecturing is big business in America today. A handful of lecture agents supply almost ninety per cent of the speakers one hears at clubs and associations, in town halls and at public meetings. The agents work a year or more ahead of the calendar, lining up engagements for their speakers; they collect as much as fifty per cent of the proceeds. They do an intensive job of publicity and personal selling, moving from convention to convention as though they were vending automobile accessories or hardware. They compete furiously for "names"—flying across the country or across the world to sign up a likely speaker on an exclusive basis. They often subtly sell their speakers' services on a tie-in basis: if the Ladies Club of Big Town, Nebraska, wants to hear a famed stage star on Saturday, June ninth, they may find it necessary to sign up an expert on The Lower Wing of the Mississippi Butterfly for Saturday, June sixteenth.

The lecture agent is almost indispensable. He "routes" the speaker so that one trip logically follows the next; so that air and railroad fares are kept to a minimum; so that the wear and tear on a man "traveling the circuit" is reduced as much as possible. But above all else, the agent is interested in "names"—people in mighty positions, people who have suddenly been discussed on Page One of the newspaper for days on end, and people who have lived *with* the "names" if the "names" themselves are no longer available.

And this is because the audience itself wants celebrities—"big" people speaking on "big" subjects, or "big" people speaking a mixture of gossip and fact. The eternal verities are somehow not nearly as attractive to the group seeking a speaker as the-girl-who-served-as-stenographer-to-the-man-who-taught-this-year's-home-run-king-to-clout-a-baseball.

Celebrities in sports, entertainment, politics, the literary field—whether or not they are good speakers—are in demand. People want to *see* them, and to be able to say they have seen them; and what the speakers actually say or how they say it is not as important.

It is difficult to make money in lecturing unless you have an agent booking you. And agents aren't going to do this unless you are a celebrity of some kind. The minister who wants to make money at lecturing these days might really consider underplaying the fact that he is a clergyman. People somehow expect that a preacher will talk without being paid!

One minister told me about the time he had made a speech without revealing his clerical identity. "After I finished speaking," he said, "the chairman of the evening arose, thanked me, complimented me, turned to his audience and said, 'Gentlemen, you have just heard what I consider to be a fine example of the thinking of America's businessmen today!' "

Lecturing sometimes invades the field of fund-raising, and a few ministers do find a certain amount of fame and fortune in this work. But again it calls for vividness as a speaker, and for a mastery of the specific techniques and appeals of the fund-raising speech. For those reasons, it offers little possibility of extra income to the average retired pastor.

The minister's best course, then, is to "work his way up" in lecturing. He usually need not go through the agony of creating a different speech for each audience; the fact is that most people who speak from the podium usually have only two speeches at best. They vary them; perhaps mix parts of one with segments of the other; and certainly change features of both to make them more applicable to the specific audiences—but in essence, two speeches they remain, and two only. The minister who perfects a stirring talk; who delivers it occasionally and at first without charge; who begins to make a "name" for himself as *the* best speaker for group meetings in his area—that minister will sooner or later come to the attention of the lecture agent. Agents scout the field with the grim earnestness of prospectors armed with Geiger-counters on a search for uranium. You can be sure you'll be found when you've reached the peak in your area! But until then, the lecture business will be no source of retirement income.

### TEACHING

Here again the possibilities of employment are slender, and the rewards not high. Age—not to mention the routine scholastic and other requirements for licensing—almost automatically rule out the possibility of a retired minister getting a teaching job in a city school system.

Perhaps the best opportunities for teaching exist in the smaller denominational colleges. Your most logical approach is to write a complete letter to the dean of such a college, outlining your training, background and experience; and telling him what subjects you feel yourself most capable of teaching, and why. It's possible that the current teacher shortage will work to your advantage; you may get a nibble. But you should be careful to check in advance the work load you will be expected to carry and the extra-curricular duties you will be asked to perform, balancing them against the salary offered and the amount of time and energy you wish to put in on a job.

You might give some thought to private teaching, or

tutoring, either on an individual basis or by organizing a class in your home.

One minister I know in a large Western city has taken advantage of the current tremendous popular interest in things religious to organize a class called "How to Read the Bible." Into his informal lectures this minister distills all the knowledge and love of the Bible he has gathered over his forty years as a minister.

Many people, he knew, tend to read the Bible almost by rote, without any real understanding of the words and the meanings behind them. His course illumines these meanings, bringing new depth to his students' understanding of the Old and New Testaments. And since he uses no denominational approach, he does not run the risk of offending anyone.

This minister built up his class by placing a few simple and inexpensive advertisements on the religious news page of his local daily newspaper. He holds the twice-a-week sessions in the spacious living-room of his house, averaging about twelve "students" per session. The "course" consists of ten weeks—twenty sessions—for twenty-five dollars, so that over every three-month period this man earns about $300. A nice sum for spare-time income!

Another minister—who was a good man in the pulpit—makes a substantial income from the public speaking courses he gives. His costs include only a minimum of advertising, some stationery and the rental of a small studio. His classes, held once a week for fifteen weeks, are usually attended by about twenty students, each of whom pays fifty dollars for the course.

One word of caution: Before attempting to set up any similar courses of instruction in medium-sized or small towns, it would be wise for you to discuss your plan with several local ministers. In this way you can make sure you will neither be intruding nor infringing. At the same time you will be acquainting them of your plans, and you may find them to be a splendid medium of publicity and an indirect source of students.

### WRITING

And now we come to writing—that great, amorphous field of enterprise in which everyone from the foreign correspondent to the housewife, from the mountaineer to the minister, thinks he can dash off a few words and make his fortune.

It isn't so.

Of course you can cite cases where unheralded unknowns have written one book and skyrocketed to success. But for every one such I can cite you thousands—yes, literally thousands—of unheralded unknowns who have written a book and *remained* "unheralded and unknown." These are the ones you do not hear about.

However—and this may come as a surprise to you—writing *can* be a source of income to the retired minister if he approaches it intelligently and diligently, and if he neither expects miracles nor bonanzas.

There are four basic areas of writing in which you can operate. Each has its own advantages and drawbacks; each its own requirements of skill; and each yields varying rewards. One reward, however, is common to them all: that is the excitement of creation, the satisfaction of completing a self-imposed task, the pride in knowing that something you have written will inform and perhaps help people.

#### I. BOOKS

Because books on religious and inspirational themes stand at the head of most best-seller lists today, the nonprofessional writer seems to think that writing such material is the fastest way to make money as an author.

Not so. As a matter of fact, it is the fastest way *not* to make money as an author. Without attempting to go too deeply into the theory and practice of the business, let me say that book publishing today is about ten per cent art and ninety per cent cost-accounting. The economics of publishing are so heavily loaded against the publisher—what with the high costs of paper, printing and distribution—that most publishers can make money only on movie sales, reprint rights, book club sales and other subsidiary sales which flow to them in part when they publish a book by a well-known author.

Most publishing houses maintain their stature as "a developer of the arts" by plowing some of their small profits back into the publishing of books by relatively unknown or new writers. But these volumes get little promotion, little buildup, and—unless they are a phenomenal surprise—little sales.

The average author of a first book is lucky if he nets as much as $500 for his efforts—efforts which generally involve a full year or more of spare-time work. And if, as a minister, you plan to write your book about a spiritual subject and aim at a limited readership to begin with, you may find your financial reward even less.

If nothing discourages you, however, then proceed with this one caution: Beware of advertisements which ask: "Do you want your book published?" Beware of those which offer "co-operative publishing" for "unknown authors." These are the standard approaches of "vanity publishers"—companies which cater to your vain wish to have your book published at any cost. In their case, "at any cost" means at *your* cost, completely or in large part. You are offered giant royalties once the book "starts to sell." But such volumes almost *never* sell—not more than a few hundred copies, in any event, and these usually to the author and his associates. A minimum publicity and promotion effort is given "vanity" titles—bookstores are wary of them, and therefore do not stock many copies of them.

I have heard of many instances in which a man wiped out his slim family fortune chasing the rainbow of fame offered by "vanity publishers"; but I know of only one or two recent instances in which real success has come to people who paid to have their books published. While there are a few honest and reasonably capable "vanity house" operations, you are best off following this general rule: If not one of the hundreds of true publishing houses in this country will take a chance on your book, odds are that it is just not publishable or marketable; and if that's the case—forget it.

Stay away too from the so-called "literary agent" who charges fees for reading your manuscript. Good agents work on a commission basis; they do not demand five dollars for reading this many thousand words, or ten dollars for that many. An unknown writer has a difficult time in finding an agent; yet he does *not* have a difficult time in placing a fine manuscript on his own. Every publisher worth his salt reads every manuscript submitted—not all the way through unless it's excellent or promising; but at least sufficiently to know whether or not it's publishable. Once again, we must say that on occasion the literary agent who charges a fee will have a flamboyant success story or two to tell; but in most of these instances it is the *product*—the story or book—which succeeded, not the agent's efforts on behalf of it. Just as the bookstores look askance at the novel published by a "vanity publisher," so do editors look askance at the manuscript submitted through a literary agent known to profit by reading fees.

*Let your work do your selling. And rely on the opinion of editors who are paid to search for authors—not those searching for authors who will pay* THEM!

You are best off if you send your manuscript directly to the publisher of your choice. Send it express prepaid, in a cardboard box; it should of course be typed, double-spaced, on good white paper; and it must always be accompanied by enough postage or money to prepay its return if it is rejected. You must allow weeks, sometimes even months to go by before you get word from the publisher. Unsolicited manuscripts such as yours pour in by the scores every day, and a publishers' reader can read only so fast. Your manuscript must wait its turn. But it will be read.

### II. MAGAZINES

This is a more promising category for the would-be writer. It is the feeling of many experienced writers and editors I know that any person with native intelligence and a command of simple English can make some money by selling ideas and articles to magazines. (This does not include magazine fiction, a highly specialized, skilled and competitive field.)

There are two categories of magazines to be considered. One is the general national magazine; the other is the religious publication. Let's discuss the latter first.

Religious publications—as you undoubtedly know—cannot pay much for the material they buy. Some of them rely completely on unpaid contributions. Others pay by the word, prices ranging from a fraction of a cent to two or three cents a word. While no one will get rich on this basis, it nevertheless can provide a steady source of income to the person who sells his work regularly.

There are two prime considerations in selling to these publications. First, the editor wants material that will teach and inspire, that will reflect spiritual values, but that will do so without being "preachy." The young people and adults who read these magazines for enjoyment as well as guidance are not going to take kindly to unalloyed moralizing.

Second, be sure that your manuscript is aimed or "slanted" properly for the market to which you are sending it. Obviously you would not send a story for young people to a publication primarily concerned with exegesis. But it is perhaps not so obvious that you ought not send a story appealing to teen-agers to a magazine edited for children of from four to eight years of age.

In the religious field there are so many magazines, pamphlets and newspapers that it would be virtually impossible to study all of them. You should, therefore, select a few for which you would like to write, and study them carefully. In most cases a brief letter to the editor or publisher will bring you an assortment of back issues of the publication. You can also ask, in the same letter, for all pertinent information about the desired lengths of manuscripts, special needs or taboos, rates of payment, and so on. You'll find that editors are more than eager to give you this information, for if they can get good material from you and others like you, the greatest of their problems will be solved.

If you write for publications in denominations other than your own, be sure you are familiar with the proper terms and traditions. Some denominations, for instance, call stewardship workers "deacons"; others refer to them as "elders"; and still others as "stewards." Be sure you use the correct terms.

The general magazine makes similar demands—but on a more competitive level. However, the work involved is worth it, for the rewards can be quite high. It is not unusual for the general magazines to pay anywhere from $300 to $1,500 per piece—and even more—for the material they buy. The price varies with the magazine, with the length and importance of the article, with the identity of the writer, and with the frequency with which a writer contributes usable material to the publication. For example, a first sale to Magazine X might bring $500, and a second piece the same amount; but the third could well be bought for $650, the fourth for $750, and so on until the magazine's top price level has been reached.

Please don't let these figures go to your head. It is difficult to sell articles to national magazines. Yet at the same time there is never enough good material available to meet the demand. I have not yet met an editor who wasn't eagerly, actively looking for material; and who wasn't willing to work hard and closely with any writer to help him develop his material properly, assuming that the writer's basic idea was interesting.

As a matter of fact, the ability to write is not of paramount importance. Roger Dakin, until recently the editor of *Collier's* Magazine, told me one day that in his opinion the ability of a contributor to come up with a *usable idea* was ninety per cent of the battle.

"If we were to pay $1,500 for a furnished article," he said, "I would consider that $1,300 of it was payment for the idea, and the other $200 was for the writing. You see," he continued, "for $200 we can get any one of a dozen competent rewrite men to edit the article. But we can't get them to think of it in the first place."

It is not the function of this book to tell you how and what to sell to the national magazines. It would not be possible, anyway, for market needs are variable and changing; ideas are highly individual and personal; and there are so many magazines which buy material at good prices that it would take a full-fledged book on this alone to cover the subject properly.

But there are several basic suggestions which can be made.

1. *Study the magazine.* You will benefit greatly if—*before you write a word!*—you take the time to browse through a year's issues of any magazine to which you ultimately plan to submit material. This browsing will give you a "feel" for the magazine, will show you what type of articles it uses, what length, and so on. It will also show you what sort of subject matter has recently been covered—subject matter you will then stay away from, so far as this magazine is concerned.

Right now it may seem to you that one "woman's" magazine is the same as any other, and that one digest-sized monthly is much like another. But you will be surprised how clearly defined are the editorial differences between, say, *McCalls* and the *Ladies Home Journal,* or *Coronet* and *Pageant.* Once you are aware of these differences and take them into consideration when submitting ideas or material, you have conquered the problem of "slanting." For "slanting" simply means sending a magazine what past history proves it wants to publish.

2. *The most salable type of article today is one that has a personal impact on the reader.* One with which the reader can identify emotionally; or one that will help him improve his income, his health, his family relations, or his attitudes. Religion and inspiration are highly marketable categories. And if you study the magazines (as has been suggested), the kind of material that has the best chance of selling will gradually become quite plain to you.

3. *An ounce of prevention is worth a pound of cure.* Many novice writers fail to take the one simple precaution that could save them much useless work: they do not check their ideas in the *Reader's Guide to Periodical Literature.* This invaluable reference book, brought up-to-date monthly with new editions, is available in virtually every public library. It lists, by subject, every article printed in some fifty major national magazines.

Thus, for example, if you suddenly decide to write an article about whales, you can check under that topic heading to see whether any stories on whales have recently been published; and if so, where. But don't let the mere listing of an article deter you. Get that copy of the magazine and read the article. Chances are you'll find that the writer talked only about whales' eating habits, for instance, whereas your idea was entirely different. You might even find some useful information in the printed article which you can quote in yours. If, on the other hand, your idea has been thoroughly covered, you might as well forget it and move on to a new one.

Not long ago I saw a man in the Public Library eagerly leafing through a volume of the *Readers Guide*. "I'm looking for something I hope I won't find," he said to me. "What's that?" I asked. "Well," he replied, "I've written a magazine article and now I want to make sure nobody's just printed it!" I couldn't help but wonder why he hadn't done this bit of research before he went to all the trouble of researching and writing his manuscript.

4. *Keep alert for ideas.* Ideas turn up in the most unlikely places and in the most unlikely ways. Many successful magazine writers insist that their most salable ideas usually develop as the result of casual conversations with friends. One writer I know sold an article entitled "Do Women Lose More Things Than Men?" simply because a friend complained that his wife was always losing her gloves, her mail, her keys, and her umbrella.

An excellent source of article ideas is the daily newspaper. Not the major stories so much as the smaller ones—those items, tucked away on the inside pages, which contain a germ of human interest. Remember, however, that these newspaper stories will give you only the jumping-off place, the starting point for an article. One writer, for example, read a newspaper story about the increase in college tuition fees expected in the next few years. He sold a magazine piece inspired by that item, but it did not follow the subject precisely, for such an article would perforce be heavily statistical and not of intense personal interest. Rather, his story was on the subject of how parents can and must plan ahead to finance their children's college education via scholarships, insurance plans, and savings *because* of the future fee increases.

Specialized magazines, company house organs and newsletters—and all similar publications dealing in material off the beaten track—often provide leads for articles. The main thing is to keep your eyes open and observant, and your mind not only receptive but actively working to convert an ordinary fact into an interesting topic. Another writer I know gets almost half of his ideas merely from reading the telephone directory. First he spots the name of a firm or a service which seems unusual; then further investigation proves whether or not it *is* unusual enough to warrant a magazine article!

*Know your markets.* It is a waste of everybody's time to send an article on child-raising to a magazine like *Popular Science,* or one on cake-baking to *Sport Magazine.* This may seem quite obvious to you; yet you would be surprised at the thousands of misdirected manuscripts editors receive each week.

There are two ways to be sure you are aiming your work in the proper direction. First, you will have studied the magazines and learned what they want and do not want. Second, you can get an up-to-date "market listing," a comprehensive rundown of all the magazines which buy free-lance material. This rundown will give you the magazine's address, the editor's name, the type and length of material he buys, and a general idea of the rates he pays and the time he takes to answer. Two of the best market guides available are the *Literary Market Place,* published by R. R. Bowker Co., New York City, and the annual *Writer's Digest Market Guide,* published by Writer's Digest Publications, Cinncinnati, Ohio.

A knowledge of markets can often pay off in several small checks rather than one large-size check if you keep in mind the possibility of selling "fillers." Fillers are brief items—anything from a two-line joke to a 500-word personal experience. The magazines use them to fill out pages, to brighten up sections, or to provide material for special departments such as *Reader's Digest's* "Life in These United States." Filler-fees range from a few dollars to $100 or more.

6. *Operate as professionally as you can.* No one can teach you how to write magazine articles, although various books and magazines can be of great help. Yet there are several basic points of editorial etiquette and mechanical know-how which we can pass on to you. They will help a great deal in smoothing your entrance into editorial rooms; by observing them, you will mark yourself as something more than a rank beginner.

a) You can save yourself much time and trouble, and at the same time please the editor, by submitting a "query" or an outline of your article idea before you actually write the piece. A query is generally a few paragraphs in length, or at the most a few pages, designed to tell the editor what your idea is, what facts and anecdotes you will present to back it up. Professional writers will simply get a "go-ahead." The neophyte will be told that the editor likes the idea, but wants to see the finished version before he definitely commits himself. It is natural for an editor to want a new writer to work "on speculation" since he cannot yet be sure the man's actual writing will measure up to his ideas. Sometimes an editor will buy the idea in your query—if you so agree—and assign a staff man or a professional writer the job of finishing it out with facts.

b) Whether you are submitting a query, a manuscript, or just a letter, it must be typewritten on white paper, double-spaced, and it should be "clean copy"—that is, not a hodge-podge of erasures, strikeovers, and corrections.

c) If you are submitting a completed manuscript, it is wise (although not necessary) to enclose a brief covering letter, or a title page giving the title of the story, your name and address, and the approximate wordage. Don't worry too much about dreaming up a bright title; nine times out of ten the editor is going to change it anyway. If you enclose a covering letter, keep it as brief as possible.

d) Leave fairly wide margins on all four sides of your paper. Start the first page halfway down, for this space will be needed for editorial markings if the piece is bought.

e) Each page should carry either your name in the upper left-hand corner, or the "slug" (identifying keyword) for the story, as well as the page number. This is a protection against loss of any page.

f) Be consistent in such things as spelling, capitalization, and punctuation, but don't worry too much about them. Each magazine has its own "style" for these things, and a purchased manuscript will be carefully edited by the staff to conform to the publication's style.

g) Never tie or sew or staple your manuscript together. Use a simple paper clip. And never try such tricks as gluing two pages together at the top to find out if the editor has read all the way through. This kind of device marks you not only as a beginner, but as a suspicious beginner. The editor can tell quite soon in your manuscript whether there is anything in it for him; if there isn't, he'll stop reading right away; if there is, he'll read on to the end.

h) Keep a carbon of your manuscript, and set up some simple record-book so you will know when you mailed the manuscript out, to whom, and when it (or a check) came back. This will prevent you from sending one article to the same publication twice. The records will also provide you with figures for income tax returns.

i) Mail your articles flat in a large envelope, accompanied by another self-addressed and stamped envelope in case of rejection. A piece of cardboard helps preserve the manuscript's appearance during its trip through the mails, often saving you a re-typing job.

j) It is a rule of the magazine profession that an article

may be submitted to only one magazine at a time. In other fields of writing this is not true: books and movie scripts, for example, may sometimes be submitted to more than one publisher or studio in the hope of arousing competitive bidding. But articles are submitted on an exclusive basis. However, you don't have to tell an editor whether your article has been previously rejected by anyone else.

Finally—and this need hardly be said—all the facts in your article must be true, accurate and the result of original thinking or original research. Plagiarism is the greatest sin, and next to it is inaccuracy. One wrong fact can involve a magazine in a potentially costly libel suit and permanently injure a magazine writer's reputation.

### III. NEWSPAPERS

The third great area of writing which can bring you financial reward lies in the daily and weekly newspaper field. The returns are not nearly so high as they can be from magazine writing, but the chances are better for making a *steady* working arrangement which can bring in small but regular sums.

The most natural area for the retired minister in journalism is the coverage of church and religious news. The big-city metropolitan papers have, of course, full staffs to cover religious events, but smaller papers often depend on part-time workers, or "stringers," to write such news stories.

If you live in a small or medium-sized town, a letter to the managing editor of the local paper may lead to a chance to show your abilities. In this letter you should briefly outline your background and offer your services as a part-time reporter or columnist responsible for church and other religious news. Since most newspaper editors shy away from "cranks," it's a good idea to state frankly in your letter that you want to do this work in order to earn extra money. Newspapermen have a healthy respect for practical men, and are much more likely to work out an arrangement with you on this basis than if you gave them some vague explanation about "wanting to be of service."

Should you get such a job, you will be responsible for rewriting and editing the releases which many churches and religious groups send out; for reporting on important events or sermons; and for other routine coverage of the religious news field. If you are good at your job, you will soon find yourself writing "feature stories" about interesting ministers, churches, parishioners, Sunday School contests, and the like. You will be paid for this work either on the basis of the time you put in; or at so much per story; or on a "string" basis, which is based on the amount of space your stories take up in the paper. If you are a "stringer" you should clip all your stories each day, paste them together into a "string," and measure them with a ruler. You are paid so much per column inch.

If you like the work and do a good job, it is entirely possible—particularly on a smaller paper—that you can work yourself into a regular staff position as religious news or church editor.

There are two important variations of this set-up. If you live in a suburb, or in a small town near enough to a large city to be considered within its shopping or trading area, you may be able to sell the small-town editor on the idea of a regular column telling the folks back home what some of their native sons are doing in the big city. This is the "country correspondent" idea in reverse.

Newspaper work of any kind puts a premium on absolute accuracy and speed. What is news today or this week is not news tomorrow or next week, and unless you are are on top of a news development at once, you might as well forget about it forever. Remember that an editor who has hired you depends on you. If you are supposed to cover a church social, or a Sunday sermon, the editor will hold space open in his paper for your report. And so you cannot suddenly decide not to cover the story because it is raining, or because you feel tired, or because Aunt Hattie has just arrived in town. If on the other hand the problem is one of illness or some other real emergency, you must notify your editor at once so that he can make arrangements to have someone present to substitute for you.

### PUBLICITY, HOUSE ORGANS, MISCELLANEOUS

The minister who has sound, practical knowledge of the writing craft can often, after retirement, earn extra income doing special types of writing jobs. For example, publicity is a prime ingredient of any fund-raising drive by a church or organization; it is integral to any special celebration by a community group such as the YMCA or the Boy Scouts. The publicity job calls for writing news and feature releases for newspapers, radio and television stations; it includes inviting reporters and photographers to cover your group's meetings or events; it requires the writing of direct-mail solicitations; and the planning of posters and decorations. Anything which can help spread the news of what your group is doing is part of the public relation man's job.

In addition, social and fraternal groups sometimes publish a regular newsletter or house organ; and while the writing and editing is often done free by a group member, some of the wealthier organizations can afford to pay salaries. These publications run the gamut from simple mimeographed-and-stapled affairs to lavishly printed booklets.

And, finally, there is the whole realm of "miscellaneous" ways in which writing can bring you money. For example, a businessman or manufacturer in your town might be extremely interested in distributing to his employees a small pamphlet on some religious or inspirational topic. A suggestion toward this end—accompanied by a sample of the sort of material you plan to write—could result in an assignment paying you several hundred dollars. In matters such as this, however, rates of payment are seldom standard. It is almost completely a question of negotiation.

Another example of "miscellaneous writing" is the writing of letters for a fee. As a minister well knows, there are in this world many lonely people; to them, a friendly and cheerful letter means a great deal indeed. And some people have made substantial sums of money by writing chatty letters at regular intervals for fees of about a dollar a letter.

Children are particularly susceptible to letters—as holiday and birthday gifts, and on other special occasions. There are services which specialize in writing letters to hospitalized or bedridden youngsters; others send a child a series of letters telling about foreign lands, or different American cities, with each letter centered about a boy or girl just like themselves.

You have to have a real flair and a real interest for this sort of enterprise to be successful at it; but the personal letter business has brought tidy sums to many retired people.

### COMMUNITY SERVICES

The man with a minister's background and reputation can find a niche with a variety of enterprises. He can, for instance, serve as chaplain to civic or community organizations; as housemaster in a private school or camp; as an adviser to youth groups; and in many other areas where his knowledge and personal responsibility make his services valuable. The only limit to the possibilities is the individual's own imagination and enterprise.

One retired minister, for example, was hired to guide an "older folks" group launched by a Washington church to provide entertainment for men and women over sixty.

Another minister turned his hobby into a fascinating service that nets him steady extra income. Too busy during his active ministerial career to read all the books he wanted to peruse, this man promised himself that after retirement he would catch up on all his deferred reading. And he did. He spent several hours of each day in the reading room of the public library, and his wide circle of friends knew it.

When, one day, one of his friends wanted to get some information in a hurry, he just naturally called the minister at the library and asked him to search for it. Soon more and more people were calling him to check facts and figures, and the minister became known around town as "Mr. Information."

Eventually his friends prevailed on "Mr. Information" to charge a small fee for his services. Today he earns much more than pocket money by charging seventy-five cents per individual question, and $1.50 an hour for lengthier research. And writers, businessmen, the local newspaper, and social workers are among his steady clients.

What will *your* imagination create for your retirement years?

*Chapter Seven*

# TESTED PART-TIME SERVICE ENTERPRISES

Experts cite a thousand and one ways in which the average man can make extra money in post-retirement small-business enterprises. Yet the plain and simple fact confronting the minister is that the very background which fits him for the creative work discussed in the previous chapter makes him more or less unfit to become an out-and-out retail merchant.

Obviously it's difficult to conceive of many clergymen able to operate, for example, a cleaning and pressing establishment, a stationery store, or a cabinet-making shop.

For one thing, it takes at least a medium amount of capital to start such a venture—more than most retired ministers are able or willing to risk. For another, it requires skills and abilities which most ministers do not have. For a third, the minister who works in his church until the very day of his retirement has no opportunity to follow the advice of retirement counselors who suggest that one "put in a little time" in getting a new venture started before retiring. And, finally, the minister usually cannot afford to wait a year or two or more to see whether his business enterprise is going to pay off.

This is the dark side of the picture. But there is a bright side, too. With imagination and ingenuity, the minister can find scores of unique and rewarding business enterprises in which he can play a part with every expectation of success. This chapter will survey a large number of such possible enterprises.

But first, here are some good, general, basic rules for anyone even considering going into a small-business operation:

*1.* Cast vanity and pride behind you—don't consider yourself "too good" to do certain kinds of work; don't look down on certain types of businesses because they seem culturally or socially "inferior." If, for example, you find you can make extra income simply by caring for pets when their owners are out of town, don't turn down the opportunity in the belief that "pet-sitting" is not consonant with the dignity of a retired minister. Dignity—as a minister above all should know—is not a matter of what a man does, but the way in which he does it.

*2.* If your business venture is in the field of small manufacture or handicrafts work, stay away from items already being mass-produced. You can never sell them for as little as your big-time competition.

*3.* If your business venture is in the field of personal service, it is by-and-large going to be restricted to the local market—the area in which you live. Therefore it is wise to study that local market intently to make sure it now can, or eventually will be able to provide a continuing demand for your services.

*4.* Be sure to make your business plans a strong factor in your decision about the place where you'll live after retirement. Opportunities vary greatly with the size, location, and makeup of a community. You may, for example, be deciding between two localities for your new home. All else being equal, the opportunities for business enterprise could well be the key factor.

*5.* Above all, never underestimate yourself. Most men never know what they can do until they do it. So don't tell yourself that you can't do this or that; remember instead that most men who retire find they can be exceedingly successful at work they never before thought they could do.

*6.* Remember, too, that you will get more out of your venture than money alone. You will sense a pride of ownership, a glow of satisfaction, and a feeling of usefulness. Best of all, you won't have time to be bored.

How shall you decide what kind of an enterprise is best for you? There are many ways. Even though you have devoted the greater part of your life to the ministry, it may be that as a youth you were trained in some other field, one to which you now can return. Skills once learned are never forgotten.

Perhaps during your years as a minister you had a hobby or an avocation—one you pursued so deeply that you became unusually skilled in it. More often than not, hobbies can be converted into money-earning business enterprises.

Perhaps your community is in need of personal services which your ministerial training makes you competent to provide—such as counseling, arbitration, and personal guidance.

Another guide to your choice of venture will be the capital required to launch it. Many ventures—particularly those in the personal service field—demand little or no investment. Others require more. Obviously the amount of money you have available to put into a business will be a determining factor in your choice.

Still another guide will be your desire or ability to work. Some enterprises can be run more or less at your will. In other words, you can work when you feel like working; and when you don't, you don't. Others must operate on steady and regular schedules lest you lose the clientele you have attracted. It's wise to stay away from fields of work demanding physical strength, long hours and close attention to details. Such a venture would defeat the very idea and purpose of your retirement. You—the retired pastor—should be able to "close up shop" whenever you feel like taking a few days off for fishing, reading or resting.

Clear thinking and the application of logic can often bring into sharp focus a money-making idea that otherwise might remain fuzzily in the background of your mind. Here, as reported by Maxwell Lehman and Morton Yarmon in "Lifetime Living" Magazine, is a good example of how one mature couple arrived at their decision.

The couple concerned were Franklin and Joan Lasker. He was a radio production man whose hobby was making sound recordings. The pressures of his high-tension business were getting too heavy for him. He and his wife were seeking a way to make a post-retirement living which would cause a minimum of strain and yet bring in a livable income. The Laskers tackled their problem with almost mathematical logic. Reported Lehman and Yarmon:

> Taking a long sheet of paper, Franklin drew a vertical line down the middle of it, dividing it into two columns. One he headed 'Franklin,' the other 'Joan.' Then on the left-hand side of the sheet he set down a number of categories: financial assets, occupational assets, hobbies, interests.
>
> Under financial assets they listed their home, which they owned free and clear, and a small 1941 Chevrolet in good running condition. They also had $250 in their joint bank account. That was all.
>
> Under occupational assets, Franklin listed: radio production man and announcer, musician (he played the piano), and bookkeeper (he had done it a long time ago). Joan listed: nursery-school teacher, housewife, cook.
>
> Under hobbies: *he,* making records: *she,* flower arrangements.

Under interests: children, clubs, theater, books, clothes, people in general.

They also listed all kinds of odds and ends that they could do, like driving a car, typing, running a mimeograph machine. And they added that both had good speaking voices.

When they had completed their chart they looked it over and came to their first conclusion: There wasn't anything in it that might give Franklin any hope of finding a job.

They went over the chart again. What combinations would be possible, out of all the things they had listed, to provide them with a living? Mr. Lasker still recalls with evident pleasure how his mind clicked away and gave him the solution: Car . . . $250 . . . nursery-school teacher . . . making recordings . . . children . . . good speaking voices.

Why, of course—that was it! They would make recordings of children's voices—be voice photographers. Both husband and wife loved children. He had the necessary recording equipment. (Such equipment can be purchased for about $200.) He and Joan had a wide acquaintance in town through their many club activities. And they decided to risk half their $250 cash for some additional tape-recording devices; small advertisements in two local newspapers; and printing up a few hundred postal cards for distribution, announcing their new voice photographer service. The car would enable them to travel to homes and record children's voices on the spot.

Mrs. Lasker promptly made use of her fine persuasive contralto. She phoned the mothers of young children she knew—and lined up six orders the first night. In each case she made appointments that would allow her husband the rest he needed.

Their first appointment was with a six-month-old baby. Franklin set up his equipment in the nursery and was soon recording the cooing, the crying and the laughter of the youngster. The child's parents were delighted; they promptly arranged a long-term deal with Franklin to record her voice every six months.

Since then Franklin has made many such arrangements. Joan keeps a card file on the birthdays of more than a thousand children, and gets in touch with the parents about a week in advance.

Gradually the business expanded. Franklin found that children's parents wanted their own voices recorded, too. Also, he got called in to make recordings of various club proceedings, meetings and symphony concerts that came over the radio. He has made a recording of a happy family at dinner, so that they might always remember their banter, their laughing good humor, with mother, father and six children participating.

Lasker's business, now several years old, is a prosperous one; and he is a happy man, doing work he enjoys.

"That's all very well," you may say, "but his was an unusual case! These two people had a number of assets which fitted together into an unusual kind of enterprise. I don't have any abilities like that."

The answer is: *Every case is an unusual case!*

If you were to sit down and make a list just as the Laskers did, it is almost impossible that you would not locate some skills or interests which could dovetail into a profitable undertaking. The biggest job is *sitting down and making the list*—and then doing realistic, constructive thinking with it.

It isn't the aim of this book to list a vast variety of *routine* small business enterprises. A walk down Main

Street and a first-person census of the shops there would probably give you the best possible list of that kind! Rather, our goal is to stimulate your imagination by telling you about some of the enterprises other people have made into constructive, satisfying and profitable sidelines. Perhaps one or more of these will strike fire in your own mind; perhaps one will point the way to some similar service or operation you can offer a community.

*Personal Services:* The field of service is a fertile one for the minister who wishes to implement his post-retirement income. Generally speaking, it does not require a wide knowledge of business practices; it does not take more time than you wish it to; it is not physically strenuous; and it often brings into play the minister's ability to work with people, rather than with manufactured articles.

"Service" is an all-inclusive word. It can cover everything from furniture-repair to starting a fine-arts lending-library. Basically a service enterprise is one in which your income is earned because of something you *do*—not because you sell a product at a price higher than its cost to you. In the latter case, you are merely a middleman. True, you perform an important function in bringing together the goods and the consumer. But in a service business you are paid for a unique ability or quality of your own.

Perhaps the simplest service business you can enter is *the creation of mailing lists.* You can earn a small but steady income from this as easily as reading your daily paper. In fact, this venture is *done* by reading your daily paper.

Lists of peoples' names are always urgently needed by mail-order houses. They use the lists to solicit business; and there is always a need for new lists. You can build up special-interest lists of names as you go through the paper. The birth announcements column will yield names for your list of new mothers and fathers—a list that any mail-order firms selling baby items will be glad to buy. From the society pages you can develop a list of new brides and brides-to-be. Names of new homeowners can be culled from the real estate pages. Young peoples' names are listed at graduation time, when entire classes see their names in print.

Your function is merely to spot the names; copy them; and be absolutely sure you have the spelling and the address copied *correctly*. You can inform mail-order firms that you have lists available by taking an inexpensive advertisement in the trade publications subscribed to by mail-order businesses; or even more simply with a series of letters.

If you keep your prices around $7.50 per thousand names, your rates will probably be enough below the rates charged by professional list houses to enable you to attract many regular customers.

As you can see, this is no get-rich-quick scheme; but it certainly is a way to get regular extra income with little extra effort.

Almost as simple is the creation of a *wrap-and-mail service*. A man in Tulsa, Oklahoma, advertised not long ago that he'd "wrap anything from false teeth to elephants for a nominal charge." And this inventive gentleman soon had as much work as he could handle! His supplies consisted of wrapping paper, corrugated paper, cardboard, string, gummed tape, and a postal scale. Armed with these and a thorough knowledge of mailing regulations, he saved his customers and the local postmaster a lot of time and trouble. Small merchants can be a fine source of repeat business in this sort of enterprise.

Here are other examples of service businesses which have been proved successful, and can be successfully adapted by you:

*Market Research:* Be it business concerns, political organizations, or study groups—everyone concerned with the public wants to know what the public is thinking! The result is that today, more than ever before, there is a continuous demand for intelligent, well-mannered and conscientious people willing to serve as part-time pollsters. And this is a field where age is an asset, for the theory is that the average person will respond more readily to a mature questioner. The chief requirement for a pollster is an ability to approach people and put his queries in an accurate, unbiased way, so that the answers will be honest and meaningful. Since market research is national in scope, every locality is a potential working area. The average pay is a dollar an hour.

Here is how you can make your availability known for this work: Get your name on file with local newspapers, the Chamber of Commerce, trade associations, and department stores; write to the market research directors of the leading advertising agencies (the list is available in the *Editor and Publisher Yearbook* at any public library); or write directly to the leading market research firms. Here are the addresses of some of the largest ones: American Institute of Public Opinion (Gallup Poll), Princeton, New Jersey; Crossley, Inc., 330 West 42nd Street, New York City, New York; Elmo Roper, 30 Rockefeller Plaza, New York City, New York.

*Errand Service:* If you have a car and like to drive, you can set up an automobile errand service for car-less neighbors. Some typical errands would be: picking up and taking home baby-sitters; making package deliveries; returning books to the library; driving youngsters to day-camp. You can charge an hourly fee sufficient to cover overhead (gas, oil, engine wear and tear, and so on) plus a small profit. Be sure you have a chauffeur's license if one is needed in your state.

*Textbook Service:* In a college town, this is an enterprise which virtually runs itself. Buy used textbooks from students at the end of a college year. Your offer to them of about a quarter of the original price will be "found money" for most undergraduates, since few students will have any further use or interest in the texts. Then, when the new semester starts, you can offer these books to new groups of students at, say, fifty to sixty percent of the original price. The differential is your profit. And unless the choice of textbooks changes, or the volumes themselves are out-dated by drastically revised editions (which usually happens only at several-year intervals) you can keep this process up as long as the textbooks are usable. You won't need to advertise, either; the college grapevine will carry your sales story quickly and efficiently.

*Book Rental Library:* Hundreds of retired men and women make good money out of the operation of their own circulating library. Once established in this field, you will be able to buy books from publishers at regular trade discounts; but it is wise to ease your way into the venture by making a working arrangement with an already-established local rental library. Offer to canvass the neighborhood for them; then make a list of the available books and start on your rounds. You should be able to develop a good bit of business for the rental library; and you'll collect a fee on all business you bring in as well as a delivery fee from your customers.

After a few months of this work you will get to know enough about your town's literary likes and dislikes so that you can open your own rental library with confidence. Two leading publishing trade journals—*Publishers' Weekly* and *Retail Bookseller*—carry frequent articles on the operation of rental libraries.

*Free-lance Office Work:* Many small businessmen have great difficulty in coping with the mass of paper-work necessary these days. Tax and payroll records, profit and loss statements, bills and invoices, letters of all kinds—these require special knowledge and special handling, and take up a tremendous amount of time. Time that most businessmen begrudge! Ministers—most of whom have kept simple church books and are expert at correspondence—can develop an excellent part-time business by taking over such chores for a few tradesmen. Usually one evening a week will suffice to do the books, answer the mail, and set up or straighten out the filing system of the small entrepreneur.

*Gardening:* Surveys have shown that the favorite hobby of most retired ministers is gardening. Here is a suggestion which can turn this hobby into a money-making service venture: a "flowers-of-the-week" club, offered from your own garden. Fresh flowers in season, attractively arranged and packaged and offered weekly at a small fee, are easily sold to local stores, civic groups, women's clubs, and private individuals. You may be able to get some customers on a monthly or seasonal contract basis.

*Selling by Telephone:* This is a good way to earn money if you are for any reason confined to home either part or all of the time. One bedridden man in San Francisco has earned over $100 a week this way for the last few years. You have to be a good salesman, though, not only to make such high earnings, *but to get the chance to make them!* First you must sell merchants on the idea of letting you do telephone solicitation for them; next you must sell products to a customer who is merely a voice on the other end of the line.

Some good items to sell by phone are house-cleaning services, fur storage, lawn and garden work, slipcovers and drapes, shows and concerts, and department-store special sales. You may be able to get a list of prospects from the merchant whom you represent; or from such organizations as women's and church groups. Otherwise you will have to work "cold" from the telephone directory. You earn a percentage of the amount of sales made. Be sure you sell only reputable goods or services for reputable concerns; you can check this beforehand with your local Better Business Bureau.

*"Talent" Pools:* The acme of personal service has been reached by a few professional men who have pooled their talents, after retirement, to form groups for consultation

and advice. This is easier for technical men to do than for men in cultural areas of work. In New York City, for example, a group of forty retired experts in industrial lines organized a management counseling service. In Schenectady, a number of retired engineers set up a drafting and consultation service on electrical and mechanical engineering problems. In Wilmington, Delaware, thirty retired business executives offer free counsel to small businessmen and to widows.

Senior Achievement Groups, a new organization, has been formed to carry this trend forward. Similar to the Junior Achievement groups—but at the other end of the age spectrum—they consist of self-organized retired persons who stake out a suitable business or service, set up production, and handle their own marketing and distribution.

*Businesses Built on Hobbies and Handicrafts:* Many a retired person has built a good business out of an activity that started merely as a hobby.

The man who is clever with his hands has a tremendously wide range of possibilities to choose from; indeed, the examples are almost endless. Let's look at just a few of the more interesting and unusual ones:

• A man in New York City who calls himself a "birdsmith" has built a fabulous business out of his hobby. When he was forced to retire, he started to whittle replicas of birds out of bits of wood. He was so fascinated by this hobby, and became so proficient at it, that he began to paint and sell his models. Today "the birdsmith" has a small shop, a backlog of orders as long as your arm, and is happily working just as much or as little as he pleases.

• In a Middle Western city, another retired man who enjoyed putting together jigsaw puzzles got bored with the simple sets he bought, and started to make his own puzzles. He buys or takes pictures of local scenic spots, glues them on to thin plywood, and cuts them into variously-shaped pieces with his electric jigsaw. Packaged in a cellophane bag, these sell speedily in local department, stationery, toy and gift stores for from fifty cents to $3.00 each.

· Using wood fiber, bits of textile, and rubber tubing, one retired Southerner keeps himself busy and makes extra money by creating artificial flowers. If you have an artistic bent, the local library has many books and articles to help you get started.

For the really handy man, various kinds of delicate repair and refinishing work often form a bridge from hobby to business. Furniture refinishing, leathercraft, metal work, a "fix-it" service for the repair of broken articles of all kinds —all these are in demand.

If you have been somewhat of a dilettante at your hobby and want to improve your technique before trying to make a business out of it, you can do the following things: check your local Board of Education for courses given in handicraft work; consult the local librarian on the subject; write to manufacturers in your particular field (makers of polishes, glues, fabrics, waxes, and so on) for whatever pamphlets or other teaching aids they may have; write to the Superintendent of Documents, U.S. Government Printing Office, Washington, D.C., for a checklist of government-published material on the subject in which you are interested.

Hobbies in foods can also be turned into remunerative part-time enterprises. Normally this field is the prerogative of women, but there are some areas in which men are just as competent. Many retired men, for example, grow mushrooms. These take little space—part of a garage or cellar— grow rapidly, require little care, and have a steady market in hotels, restaurants and food stores. In addition the U.S. Government has a number of licensed Mushroom Receiving Stations which buy mushrooms for resale. The U.S. Agriculture Department has many inexpensive publications about mushrooms, as do a number of seed companies.

Herbs and spices are another food hobby one can build into a part-time business. They can be grown in small home gardens and even marketed from there. Generally more lucrative, however, is the field of medical herbs, roots and barks. These can be gathered in woods and fields, and resold in their natural state to wholesale drug firms. Deer-tongue leaves, slippery elm bark, pumpkin seeds, ginseng and hydrangea roots—these are all in steady demand.

All regions of the country contribute some varieties of these plants. The U.S. Farm Bureau agent in your locality, or the state agricultural department, has pamphlets to help teach you where to look for these plants and how to recognize them. Many government pamphlets are available on the subject, as well as books in the library. For a summary of how to make money as a herb-gatherer—along with a list of current price levels—write to S. B. Penick & Co., Asheville, North Carolina.

*Pets:* If you like animals (and animals like you), another new field for part-time money-enterprises is open to you. Pets can be profitable in many ways. You can breed them, board them, or "baby sit" with them.

If you can buy or build inexpensive facilities, you can create a year-round business in taking care of dogs, cats and other pets while their families go away on vacation trips. Or, if you have a car, you can feed and care for the animals in their own homes. One woman I know visits about six "clients" a day, ranging from goats to goldfish.

Animal breeding is far more difficult, requiring expert knowledge and constant care, but its financial rewards can be larger. If you go in for temperamental creatures like chinchillas or mink, your troubles and your income can be big. But there are many animals you can raise more easily: fish, rabbits, canaries, mice, guinea pigs, or pheasant. You are most likely to have a successful enterprise if you breed an animal for which there is a steady demand. Many small mammals are needed on medical research projects: hunting clubs buy thousands of pheasant and other game birds; and earthworms—for bait, for zoo food and as soil conditioners

—can be a fabulous business. It is not unusual for an original investment of $10 or $20 (which buys about 2,000 breeding earthworms) to burgeon into a $5,000 business within a few years. Your best source for information on this enterprise is your state agricultural college extension service.

*Mail-Order Businesses:* One of the great American dreams seems to be a vision of the postman calling at our door each day with a bagful of envelopes stuffed with dollar bills—each an order for our home-grown shampoo, our new booklet, our special dustcloth, or our blackberry preserves.

This is the great vision of the mail-order businessman. And quite often it comes true. As a nation, America buys billions of dollars worth of products and services through the mails each year. We pay these billions to large mail-order firms (like Sears, Roebuck and Montgomery Ward); to medium-sized ventures; and to individuals—housewives, craftsmen, and retired people.

Obviously, therefore, this is a field for you to consider. You should enter it with caution, however, and only after thorough planning and preparation, since there are as many failures in the the mail-order business as there are successes. But it can be a remarkably easy-going way of earning a fair amount of extra cash after retirement if you follow the advice of experts.

Success depends primarily on four factors: (1) your product or service; (2) your presentation and approach; (3) the ability to keep your price low; and (4) the quality of your mail-order lists.

A casual glance through magazines and newspapers reveals an incredible range of goods and services offered. Everything from food-warmers to correspondence courses—from dolls and vitamins to underwear and prefabricated garages—is for sale by mail. Thus arises the first question: Is there anything left for you to sell?

A top authority on mail-order business is Maxwell B. Sackheim of New York City. He told one reporter:

"The need for mail-order is never-ending. Mail-order decentralizes selling, makes for easy shopping. In mail-order buying, the customer can stay at home."

Another expert, discussing mail-order as a field for retired persons, said:

"It all depends on the individual. He must be able to develop a trial-and-error system; he must not be afraid to experiment. He must be flexible—prepared to move from one product to another, or to change the price if this seems advisible. But age by itself is certainly no barrier to success in mail-order."

If you can offer a unique product or service at a reasonable price—something that no one else can offer or has yet thought of offering—you have the greatest single asset for success. An example is the excellent business built up by a man in Maine who sells live lobsters by mail. His unique idea was a packaging method which allowed him to freeze the lobsters in a new and superior way.

The next best thing is to have a product or service you can honestly advertise as being better than any similar one. A man in California has been selling his own perfume by mail quite successfully for many years. Thousands of women like it better than the well-known brands.

The third best thing is to be able to offer an ordinary item at a lower price than is usual.

If you are contemplating the mail-order business, check the U.S. Department of Commerce for a list of products and services which tend to sell well and consistently over long periods. Here are some such *products:*

Unusually-designed jewelry; automobile accessories; arch supporters and exercise equipment; plants, shrubs, seeds, and garden implements; shirts and ties; toys, puzzles and novelties; home-craft tools; stamps and coins; photographic accessories; knocked-down furniture or specially-finished furniture; all sorts of household cleaning items; homemade food; stationery, desk and office supplies.

Here are *services* which have proved to be mail-order successes:

Secretarial (addressing, mailing, typing, proofreading, mimeographing, editing, and writing); commercial art work and photo developing; correspondence courses of all kinds.

Remember, you do not have to be able to make the goods or offer the service yourself. Most mail-order businessmen buy the products or contract for the services, and make their profit on the differential between their cost and the sales price. So it may require some working capital to get started. But it certainly doesn't take as much as other businesses do.

Surveys show that about one-third of all mail-order businesses were started with a capital of $500 or less, while another third required an original investment of from $500 to $3,000. Earnings range from a few dollars to several hundred dollars a month; much depends on the energy with which you pursue this part-time business. The average income from a moderately successful, one-man, part-time mail-order business is between $1,000 and $2,000 a year.

Mail-order has an additional advantage in that you can start it in as small a way as you wish, and expand gradually as your product or service catches on. If it does not catch on, your loss of time and money is small, and you are in a flexible enough position to be able to switch to some other item.

Once you start, you must be sure of a continuous source of supply. You don't want to overstock, yet you must be able to meet the orders. This means that you must be able to get your goods regularly and steadily, at a fixed, agreed-to price. Your price to the buyer should net you at least ten percent profit after you have met the cost of all your overhead.

What will this overhead include? Well, the cost of the item you are selling; your own time; costs of mailing and advertising; perhaps the cost of lists of names to circularize, or fees to someone who will write your sales letters; and costs of packaging your product.

Two cautions: (1) some items may be subject to Federal

regulations regarding food, drugs and cosmetics—you had better check the legal aspects if you are considering selling such items; (2) there are Post Office regulations to be met.

But in general there is no licensing necessary, a minimum of red tape, and a maximum of stimulating opportunity in mail-order business ventures.

Libraries are filled with good books giving advice on the field, and both the U.S. and your State Departments of Commerce will be glad to help.

If you are serious about considering some kind of business venture as a post-retirement hedge against boredom and lack of money, you would do well to make as early a start as possible in planning. Here are some things you can and should do immediately upon your retirement, or, if possible, before you retire:

Decide as definitely as you can what you want to do. Base your decision on your aptitudes, interests, health, financial needs, and the area in which you will be living.

Read and study all you can about the field you hope to enter. The U.S. Government is a gold-mine of a source. The Bureau of Information of the Department of Commerce, Washington, D. C., has scores of booklets on small business operations, as well as information bulletins updating this material and giving further sources of information.

Ask your public librarian to show you the many business-help books on her library shelves.

Make use of the many business trade associations which issue advisory bulletins; and read the appropriate trade papers and magazines.

Think about taking one of the adult-education courses now offered in public schools (many at night, and some by mail). These help mature persons develop skills and increase their background knowledge in specialized fields.

*Chapter Eight*

# CHOOSING A PLACE TO LIVE AFTER RETIREMENT

One of the great freedoms which comes with retirement is the freedom to choose the place where you will live. Men are generally tied to a location by their work; and while ministers may perhaps do more moving about during their working years than other men, they move in response to the call of a congregation—not in joyful answer to the call of mountain air or a fishing lake.

After years of living in a place simply because that's where one's work happens to be, the opportunity to live in a place because one *wants* to live there is somewhat overwhelming. Like the chance to eat candies and sweets after years of a sugar-free diet, it's hard to determine which to taste first!

As in all other aspects of wise retirement, however, careful advance thinking and planning will help overcome many problems. Retired ministers usually do not have the economic resources to make the "exploratory" trips to other communities so often recommended by experts on retirement; by the time they had passed a few months here and a few months there, surveying one area after another, they might very well have exhausted their retirement "nest-egg." The minister and his wife, therefore, must often do their relocation planning during vacation trips; or vicariously, by reading about logical retirement areas. After having gathered as many facts as they can in this way, the couple should then decide firmly what is important to them in locale—and what "tests" they will apply to likely spots for permanent living.

This is not nearly so difficult as it may sound. Most of the "tests" are simple, logical questions. Here, for example, are several of the more important ones; and others will occur to you as you begin to think over the problem of location in terms of your individual preferences, needs, and problems.

*1.* To a minister, the list may well be topped by the question: *Will there be enough opportunity for me to supply pulpits?* Isolated and inaccessible areas, while charming and peaceful, are certainly not going to put you near a large number of churches to be supplied. And so you may choose to settle in or near an area where you are well-known, where your denomination is strong, and where you have friends in the ministry who will think of you promptly if supply opportunities arise.

2. *Is the climate healthful and pleasant?* A warm climate—one which avoids extremes of range and sudden changes of temperature—will not only be beneficial physically, but financially as well. For instance, older bodies need less food in warm areas; there is no need for a multiplicity of winter coats and suits, gloves and mufflers and snowshoes; the exertions involved in putting on and taking off these clothes is avoided, along with the need to shovel snow and drain cellars; houses need no heat, or little heat; and inexpensive out-of-door living can be the rule rather than the exception.

*3. Are the living costs high?* As we have seen in an earlier chapter, living costs for older persons usually vary from locality to locality, much of the variance being due to differences in housing costs. The price of food; the cost and availability of houses and apartments; the number and amount of local taxes—all these elements are prime considerations in selecting a place for retirement.

*4. Will you be near friends or family?* You may not want to stick too close to relatives or to friends—but you don't want to cut yourself off from them geographically, either! Many couples who have retired to climate-perfect Hawaii, for instance, say that the only trouble with living there is that it takes so much time and money to get home to the mainland, or for friends and family to visit them.

*5. Does the locale offer opportunities for earning extra income?* Is it an area of heavy unemployment, or does it have more jobs than workers? Are there activities (such as tourism) which lend themselves to the creation of profitable part-time enterprises?

*6. Does it provide opportunities for the kind of hobbies you enjoy?*

*7. How will it affect your health?* Apart from climate, other factors are involved—for example, the medical facilities available. You may not feel comfortable living in a town which does not have a modern hospital and does not offer a wide choice of doctors and nurses.

*8. Will it stimulate you intellectually?* Retirement does not mean dormancy. You still want good talk, interesting ideas, and the chance to appreciate cultural experiences. Many towns which can brag about their good fishing and their good food certainly cannot boast about their museums or lectures, their concerts or plays, their libraries or adult education classes.

*9. Does it have what you require spiritually?* Obviously you want to live in an atmosphere of wholesomeness. You will want to know what churches there are, how well they are attended, and certainly whether there is a good church of your own faith in operation.

*10. Is it accessible?* Not every town is going to be able to answer each of these questions positively. Indeed, some of these "tests" are mutually exclusive. But a town that is accessible by rapid and inexpensive transportation to other areas can make up for many lacks. If a half-hour train ride on a suburban train can bring you to a cultural center, that is certainly just as good as having Carnegie Hall next door.

Accessibility is vital. Too many retiring couples automatically dream of going to live in a rural hamlet. True, such areas offer advantages: the cost of living is lower; life is informal and friendly; you can more readily supplement your income or your larder with a vegetable garden or by fishing in the nearby trout stream; and often rural areas are vacation or tourist-centers, enabling you to set up such income-producing establishments as motels, gift shops, or equipment-rental stores. But on the other hand, the man who falls in love with the lakes and woodlands and the isolated cabin often finds out too late that he would much rather have fewer trees and more food stores, laundromats, drugstores, doctors—and just plain people to talk to.

With these questions as guideposts, you can do some serious thinking about where you will live after retirement. *Do it seriously, please!* You won't want to make more than one move. A change of location is a rude enough upheaval to your body and your mind without forcing yourself to submit to it more than once. No change of location should be made so suddenly, furthermore, that you do not have a chance to prepare for it by gradual shifting of your interests and activities.

When you come right down to it, personal preferences on little things are going to prove the dominant factors in your choice and your decision. Since nothing is more certain than that individual vagaries are virtually infinite, it is hardly practicable to pinpoint the advantages and disadvantages of every potential retirement locality. In the remaining pages of this chapter, therefore, we'll survey the *major* areas most popular and most logical for retired older persons. After this birds-eye view, you'll be better fitted to pick your spots.

Because reasonable costs of living and equability of climate are the two most important factors for most older persons, six sections of our nation have developed into the most-favored areas for retirement living. They are the Atlantic Seaboard; Florida; the Ozarks; the Gulf Coast; the Southwest; and California. Let us look at each of these.

### THE ATLANTIC SEABOARD

Admittedly, this takes in a huge chunk of territory, but since for the most part retirement areas are coastal areas, we are actually talking about that thin strip of seacoast land running from New England down through the Middle Atlantic States to the northern boundary of Florida—which is a story all to itself.

*New England:* Friends of the area call it an "invigorating climate"; detractors call it a harsh one. Yet New England offers advantages to the retired person which may well offset the bluster and snow of its winters.

It has restful scenery; people whom you may get to know slowly but extremely well; nooks and crannies in the mountains of the interior, along the myraid lakes, or clinging precariously to the rugged coast, making quiet backwaters for retirement. Costs for heating and clothing are high; costs for food are medium; and costs for housing are among the lowest in the country. Old houses and old farms—some of them long-abandoned and indubitably needing a good bit of repairs—can often be picked up for astonishingly small sums. And these prices make feasible the spending of some additional money on repairs.

A tourist mecca—especially in the summer, for its swimming and boating; and in the fall, for its magnificent foliage season—New England also offers countless opportunities for spare-time income-producing businesses. It has the advantage of being close to Boston and New York, two metropolitan centers; and it has many cultural centers of its own, with special emphasis on music and dance festivals. For those interested in cultural pursuits, college towns—with their faculties, courses, libraries, and intellectually stimulating atmosphere—abound.

Massachusetts—key state of the New England complex—seems to be particularly fertile ground for ministers wishing pulpit work. Here is what Lenox E. Bigelow, general representative of the Department of Commerce of the Commonwealth of Massachusetts, told us:

> We find, after a careful check of the various Protestant denominational associations, that retired ministers find Massachusetts a desirable region to live in.
>
> The largest concentration appears to be in the Metropolitan Boston area, in any of the several dozen communities you might wish to mention. This, we understand, is particularly true of retired ministers wishing to supply pulpits or act as interim pastors.
>
> We checked with the Massachusetts Congregational Conference, and a list of nearly one hundred retired ministers of that denomination revealed the great majority in the Boston area, but the minority well scattered in other communities—mostly the smaller ones—throughout the Commonwealth.
>
> Cape Cod and Martha's Vineyard Island, and towns in western Massachusetts, were the residences of quite a large number. The smaller communities seem to attract many, as living costs are somewhat less than in the cities and there is an opportunity for closer association with the residents.

## THE EAST

| TEMPERATURES | Jan-Feb | | Mar-Apr | | May-June | | July-Aug | | Sept-Oct | | Nov-Dec | |
|---|---|---|---|---|---|---|---|---|---|---|---|---|
| | AM | PM | AM | PM | AM | PM | AM | PM | AM | PM | AM | PM |
| Boston | 36 | 20 | 49 | 33 | 70 | 53 | 79 | 62 | 66 | 50 | 44 | 30 |
| New York | 38 | 24 | 50 | 36 | 70 | 57 | 86 | 66 | 69 | 54 | 46 | 33 |
| Portland | 31 | 16 | 45 | 31 | 61 | 50 | 75 | 60 | 63 | 47 | 40 | 26 |
| Washington | 42 | 27 | 58 | 39 | 79 | 59 | 85 | 67 | 73 | 53 | 50 | 33 |

| DAYS WITH RAIN | Jan | Feb | Mar | Apr | May | June | July | Aug | Sept | Oct | Nov | Dec |
|---|---|---|---|---|---|---|---|---|---|---|---|---|
| Boston | 12 | 10 | 12 | 11 | 11 | 10 | 10 | 10 | 9 | 9 | 10 | 11 |
| New York | 12 | 10 | 11 | 11 | 11 | 11 | 11 | 10 | 9 | 9 | 9 | 11 |
| Portland | 12 | 11 | 9 | 11 | 12 | 12 | 12 | 11 | 10 | 9 | 11 | 11 |
| Washington | 11 | 10 | 12 | 11 | 11 | 11 | 11 | 11 | 8 | 8 | 9 | 10 |

### THE MIDDLE ATLANTIC STATES

This region includes one of the most popular retirement areas in the United States: that section comprising Virginia, the two Carolinas, and Georgia.

The climate is truly moderate: warmer in the winter than New England, cooler in summer than Florida and the Gulf South. Along the coast, "cold snaps" are infrequent and brief, and snow is almost non-existent; further back in the hilly interior, snow is rare and winters are bracing without being bitter. Summer heat is lowered by the higher altitudes in the interior.

The range of living is tempting and varied. There are college towns (not as many as in New England); congenial communities made up almost entirely of retired persons; small communities off the main highways (but not so far off as to be inaccessible), where neither land nor housing is costly, and where food is either cheap to buy or relatively simple to raise yourself.

Indeed, in almost all ways the Middle Atlantic area is keynoted by the word "moderation."

The Carolinas have one unusual climatic condition of interest to retiring persons. That is its "thermal belts." According to the U.S. Weather Bureau, a thermal belt is an area where certain atmospheric conditions combine "to cause the temperature on the slope of a mountain range to be from one to fourteen degrees higher than at the top of the mountain or at the bottom."

Living in a thermal belt gives you the advantage of warmer winters, but also the disadvantage of warmer summers.

The Middle Atlantic States are ideally situated for anyone who wants "to get away from it all" but also wants to be able to get *back* to it quickly if the occasion arises. With excellent train and plane service available, it is scarcely more than an overnight trip, at most, from North Carolina to so wide a variety of metropolitan centers as New York, Chicago, and Detroit.

Two examples—at the extremes—will suffice to give you an idea of the range of retirement living available in this area. At one end of the scale is a town like Southern Pines, famous (if for nothing else) for the fact that nine top-ranking retired generals chose it as their retirement home. Activities center about the golf course, horse shows and a fairly formal social life. Living, as you may imagine, is rather expensive, with even small houses priced at no less than $8,000.

At the other extreme are the communities of the Outer Banks—a chain of coastal islands that are for the most part undeveloped. The government recently established part of this area as the country's newest National Park. Many of the islands are populated by fishermen; there is no local government and no local taxes; and despite their exposed position, the Outer Banks have a fairly mild climate thanks to the proximity of the Gulf Stream. Living is simple, basic, and cheap.

### FLORIDA

More retired persons choose Florida as the home of their later years than any other place in the United States. Florida's only competition as the land of peace and relaxation comes from California; but each year sets a new record for the number of families who move to Florida to become permanent residents. There are now about 300,000 retired people who own homes in the state.

What are the reasons for Florida's popularity?

First, of course, its climate. Florida is farther south than any other state. In its southern area the plant and animal life begins to approximate the sub-tropical. Yet the water which virtually surrounds the entire state keeps temperatures at a pleasant average of from 68 degrees in January to slightly over 80 degrees in July. Even at the height of the summer the cooling night breezes and the short afternoon rains keep the heat from becoming oppressive. The abundance of sunshine, the balminess of the air and the relatively mild and damp atmosphere combine to create a climate that is physically relaxing to older persons.

The bugaboo of hurricanes is vastly overrated. U.S. Weather Bureau statistics show that the odds of a hurricane-force wind striking in any given year range from one in seven at Miami and the Keys, to one in thirty at Daytona Beach. The chances are even less as you go up the coasts. In recent years weather experts have found that Caribbean-born hurricanes are taking a new course which usually swerves them even farther away from the Florida coast.

A second reason for Florida's popularity is its relatively low cost of living. Housing runs about thirty to forty percent cheaper, either to build or buy, than it does in Northern states. A house or a lot can be bought within the limits of almost any budget. Many folks become trailerites after a visit to Florida because of the large number of luxurious and inexpensive trailer camps in operation there. Some buy a lot, park their trailer on it, build a small house, and then sell the trailer!

Several factors contribute to this low cost of housing. Homes need no basements (a substantial construction economy), and little in the way of heating plants. Consequently, construction material can be as cheap as concrete block.

Crops grow readily in Florida, and many retired couples raise large amounts of food for their own use without difficulty or undue exertion. If you live on the coast, fishing provides another source of free food. Local groves provide an inexpensive source of citrus fruits.

## THE SOUTH

| TEMPERATURES | Jan-Feb AM | Jan-Feb PM | Mar-Apr AM | Mar-Apr PM | May-June AM | May-June PM | July-Aug AM | July-Aug PM | Sept-Oct AM | Sept-Oct PM | Nov-Dec AM | Nov-Dec PM |
|---|---|---|---|---|---|---|---|---|---|---|---|---|
| Atlanta | 53 | 36 | 67 | 47 | 83 | 64 | 87 | 70 | 77 | 60 | 57 | 45 |
| Charleston | 59 | 37 | 69 | 54 | 83 | 69 | 88 | 75 | 79 | 66 | 63 | 48 |
| Miami | 75 | 61 | 79 | 65 | 85 | 73 | 88 | 76 | 85 | 73 | 77 | 64 |
| New Orleans | 64 | 48 | 74 | 58 | 86 | 71 | 90 | 76 | 83 | 69 | 67 | 56 |

| DAYS WITH RAIN | Jan | Feb | Mar | Apr | May | June | July | Aug | Sept | Oct | Nov | Dec |
|---|---|---|---|---|---|---|---|---|---|---|---|---|
| Atlanta | 12 | 11 | 11 | 10 | 9 | 11 | 12 | 12 | 8 | 7 | 8 | 11 |
| Charleston | 9 | 9 | 9 | 7 | 8 | 11 | 13 | 13 | 10 | 6 | 7 | 9 |
| Miami | 8 | 6 | 7 | 7 | 11 | 13 | 15 | 15 | 18 | 15 | 10 | 8 |
| New Orleans | 10 | 9 | 9 | 7 | 9 | 13 | 15 | 14 | 11 | 7 | 7 | 10 |

There is no state income tax, and other taxes are quite low.

The third reason for Florida's popularity is the state's concern for the older person. Newcomers are welcomed. Several communities have gone into large-scale, low-cost housing projects tailored to meet the needs of retired or older persons. Some offer "package plans" which include community stores, community gardens, community recreation, and other cooperative ventures; these help immeasurably in cutting costs, permitting an older person to budget ahead effectively. Another aspect of the state's concern for older persons is the continuing investigation which state agencies make into problems of the retired or aging person.

The flood of tourist business, of course, offers almost endless opportunity for part-time ventures. And the state's emphasis on the welfare of older folk has made it possible to obtain part-time work more readily than might be the case elsewhere. Many small industrial plants hire retired persons in supervisory jobs; many areas are set up specifically to give older persons a chance to be gainfully employed for part of the time.

Geographically, the state offers a wide range of locations for settling—from the mossy forest lands of the north through the pinelands and the orange groves of the central section to the palm-treed beaches of the south. And down the center of the state runs the lake country—rich farmland and small commercial towns nestled in a hilly area where over 30,000 lakes have already been counted.

The large number of communities in the state means there are a large number of churches—and they are well-attended by the older persons who comprise such a large proportion of the total population. This, in turn, means a wider opportunity for pulpit supply work.

### THE GULF COAST

This stretch of land sweeps in a semi-circular arc around the Gulf of Mexico, and extends from northwestern Florida across Alabama, Mississippi and Louisiana. In many ways it offers retirement advantages similar to those of Florida. But there are enough differences to qualify it as a section of its own.

The climate is somewhat cooler than Florida's throughout the year, but certainly mild by Northern standards. Summer highs average in the low 80's, and winter lows seldom get below the 50's. Humidity is low; cloudy days rare; and rainfall more showery than stormy.

This means, in turn, that housing is relatively inexpensive, just as it is in Florida. Slightly higher heating costs are the rule, and you'll experience occasional need for a winter overcoat; but in general, living costs are reasonable. Food prices are low, with vegetables easily grown year-round. And fish and shellfish are so plentiful that in many communities they are sometimes given away to prevent spoilage.

The Gulf Coast way of life is unique—a combination of indolence and graciousness which evidences the influence of the French and Spanish who used to control it. The Gulf Coast has not yet had the large influx of retired persons which other areas have experienced; many of its residents are local people who have made the break from the big cities of the South—either permanently or on a "summer vacation" basis.

But one unique attribute of the area is sure to attract growing numbers of older persons. That is the "ozone belt" —a region of Louisiana which takes in about a dozen towns near New Orleans. Ozone is a purer form of oxygen, produced by the silent discharge of electricity in the air. The ozone belt is characterized by pine forests; deep artesian wells yielding water of extreme purity; medical springs of therapeutic value (which occur in many sections of the Gulf Coast); and a uniformly mild climate.

The ozone belt is particularly recommended for sufferers from respiratory ailments and diseases of the heart. There's a story (probably apochryphal) about a couple from Louisiana who visited one spa after another, and medical experts all over Europe, in an effort to ease their respiratory troubles. Finally one doctor told them of a town where the air alone effects a cure for almost all respiratory diseases. "Where is this town?" the couple asked anxiously. "Why," said the doctor, "it's in Louisiana!"

As a clincher, here are some Government statistics: The death rate for the United States is 14.67 per 1,000. The death rate in the ozone belt is 9.3 per 1,000. Chief localities in the ozone belt are Slidell, Covington, and Abita Springs, Louisiana.

### THE OZARKS

In the American Midwest, where summer temperatures climb over the 100° mark frequently, and winters are marked by blizzards and cold waves, the Ozark Mountain area of Arkansas lies like an enclave of moderation. Because of its equable climate and its extremely low-cost living, this area is gradually coming to the fore as a prime retirement region. Its chief drawback for the retiring minister could well be its comparative cultural isolation.

Climate-wise, the region is a "four season" one, with winter and summer both short, and spring and fall quite long. An extremely low average humidity makes the area especially pleasant for those troubled by rheumatic ailments.

Almost seventy percent of the people of Arkansas live on farms or in towns with populations under three thousand. This makes for a lack of bustle and tension in everyday living; a peacefulness many seek after a crowded, event-filled career.

Living costs are quite low. One expert has said that a

## CENTRAL

| TEMPERATURES | Jan-Feb | | Mar-Apr | | May-June | | July-Aug | | Sept-Oct | | Nov-Dec | |
|---|---|---|---|---|---|---|---|---|---|---|---|---|
| | AM | PM | AM | PM | AM | PM | AM | PM | AM | PM | AM | PM |
| Chicago | 33 | 19 | 49 | 35 | 70 | 55 | 80 | 66 | 67 | 53 | 42 | 29 |
| Dallas | 57 | 38 | 71 | 51 | 86 | 67 | 94 | 75 | 83 | 63 | 61 | 43 |
| St. Louis | 41 | 25 | 59 | 41 | 80 | 62 | 87 | 70 | 74 | 56 | 48 | 32 |

| DAYS WITH RAIN | Jan | Feb | Mar | Apr | May | June | July | Aug | Sept | Oct | Nov | Dec |
|---|---|---|---|---|---|---|---|---|---|---|---|---|
| Chicago | 11 | 10 | 12 | 11 | 12 | 11 | 9 | 9 | 9 | 9 | 10 | 11 |
| Dallas | 8 | 8 | 7 | 8 | 9 | 7 | 5 | 6 | 5 | 6 | 6 | 7 |
| St. Louis | 9 | 9 | 11 | 11 | 11 | 11 | 8 | 8 | 8 | 8 | 8 | 9 |

retired couple can live in Arkansas and be well-fed, well-clothed and well-housed on $1,500 a year. In many areas an income of $125 a month would be sufficient to finance a very comfortable way of life. Food is cheap, since the state produces an abundance of every food staple, with much buying being done directly from farmers. Supplemented by home gardens and a berrypatch, your food purchases will likely be below $40 a month. Both housing and land are extremely low-priced.

Arkansans, always tourist-conscious, are beginning to realize the value of new permanent residents as well. State leaders, aware of the desirability of retired couples as new citizens, are planning a series of steps to stimulate "immigration" by making the state's assets even more appealing.

### THE SOUTHWEST

Arizona and New Mexico provide retirement opportunities in an area where the casual, outdoor life predominates. The climate varies considerably with the topography. In the altitudinous northern sections of the state, the winters are likely to be cold and the summers pleasantly warm; in the valleylands of the south, winters are warmer, but summer temperatures often climb into the high 90's and 100's. The dry air, however, keeps the heat quite bearable. Low humidity and almost constant sunshine combine to make the Southwest beneficial for those suffering from respiratory or rheumatic ailments.

The cost of living varies, but in general it is probably somewhat higher than for comparable areas in Florida or along the Atlantic seacoast. Much food has to be brought in over long distances; and housing accommodations have been tightened by the rapid rise in populations. On top of this, both states report an oversupply of workers, and warn that retiring couples must be assured of their incomes from investments or pensions, because the opportunities to earn

## ROCKIES AND SOUTHWEST

| TEMPERATURES | Jan-Feb | | Mar-Apr | | May-June | | July-Aug | | Sept-Oct | | Nov-Dec | |
|---|---|---|---|---|---|---|---|---|---|---|---|---|
| | AM | PM | AM | PM | AM | PM | AM | PM | AM | PM | AM | PM |
| Albuquerque | 50 | 24 | 66 | 36 | 83 | 53 | 89 | 62 | 77 | 48 | 53 | 36 |
| Denver | 44 | 20 | 55 | 31 | 75 | 49 | 85 | 56 | 71 | 44 | 49 | 24 |
| Phoenix | 67 | 41 | 78 | 50 | 96 | 64 | 102 | 77 | 91 | 62 | 70 | 44 |
| Salt Lake City | 38 | 20 | 56 | 34 | 77 | 48 | 91 | 60 | 72 | 44 | 44 | 25 |

| DAYS WITH RAIN | Jan | Feb | Mar | Apr | May | June | July | Aug | Sept | Oct | Nov | Dec |
|---|---|---|---|---|---|---|---|---|---|---|---|---|
| Albuquerque | 3 | 3 | 3 | 4 | 4 | 3 | 8 | 8 | 5 | 4 | 2 | 3 |
| Denver | 5 | 6 | 8 | 9 | 10 | 8 | 9 | 9 | 6 | 6 | 5 | 5 |
| Phoenix | 4 | 4 | 4 | 2 | 1 | 1 | 5 | 6 | 3 | 2 | 2 | 4 |
| Salt Lake City | 10 | 10 | 9 | 9 | 7 | 4 | 4 | 6 | 4 | 7 | 7 | 8 |

extra income are not widespread. Nevertheless, many retired couples do quite well financially with such part-time businesses as leathercraft, gem carving, and so on.

For example, one retired minister, Dr. A. F. Wasson, makes a good income from his overnight guest ranch near Taos. Dr. and Mrs. Wasson operate their ranch during the two tourist-busy summer months, and live the life of retirement the other ten months.

Much of the recreational activity is likely to be more energetic than in the East, with a good deal of emphasis on hunting, fishing, hiking, skiing and boating.

Arizona reports a seventy percent rise in the over-forty age group during the past ten years, and an eighty-five percent rise in the over-sixty-five age group. Perhaps the chief reason for this influx of older couples are the health-giving properties of the climate—once described as a "catalyst which helps to stimulate the natural sources of energy."

And a big part of the Southwest's success as a haven is due to the natural friendliness of its people—warm-hearted, hospitable, and ready to go out of their way to be helpful to newcomers.

### CALIFORNIA

Here is Florida's standout rival for the title of "retirement capital of the United States." Every day literally hundreds of newcomers pour into the state to live out their years in the ease of its pleasantness.

Its size and its geography give California great advantages to offer retiring persons. There is, for example, a wide range of climate. Along the southern coast, temperatures vary from the mid-50's during the winter to the mid-70's during the summer, with cooling on-shore breezes keeping the heat down. Humidity is low and rain (despite the jokes about California weather) quite infrequent.

Temperatures drop as you proceed northwards up the coast, but never get very low, thanks to the stabilizing in-

## WEST COAST

| TEMPERATURES | Jan-Feb | | Mar-Apr | | May-June | | July-Aug | | Sept-Oct | | Nov-Dec | |
|---|---|---|---|---|---|---|---|---|---|---|---|---|
| | AM | PM | AM | PM | AM | PM | AM | PM | AM | PM | AM | PM |
| Los Angeles | 65 | 47 | 69 | 50 | 74 | 55 | 82 | 60 | 78 | 57 | 70 | 50 |
| San Francisco | 57 | 46 | 61 | 49 | 65 | 52 | 65 | 58 | 68 | 59 | 60 | 49 |
| Seattle | 47 | 37 | 55 | 41 | 66 | 50 | 73 | 55 | 63 | 50 | 49 | 40 |

| DAYS WITH RAIN | Jan | Feb | Mar | Apr | May | June | July | Aug | Sept | Oct | Nov | Dec |
|---|---|---|---|---|---|---|---|---|---|---|---|---|
| Los Angeles | 6 | 7 | 6 | 4 | 2 | 1 | 0 | 0 | 1 | 2 | 3 | 6 |
| San Francisco | 11 | 11 | 10 | 6 | 4 | 2 | 1 | 1 | 2 | 4 | 7 | 10 |
| Seattle | 18 | 16 | 16 | 13 | 12 | 9 | 4 | 5 | 8 | 13 | 17 | 18 |

fluence of the Pacific Ocean. Fog, however, can be a problem in the San Francisco area.

In the lush interior valleys of the state, summer temperatures go high, but the dryness of the air does much to mitigate the heat.

As with climate, so with everything else—a wide range to choose from. A Californian can literally drive within a few hours from one of the world's finest bathing beaches to one of the world's finest ski resorts—and find everything else in between. Housing can range from expensive homes in La Jolla to rustic cabins in the Marin County woods, from beach houses to forest homes.

Income-producing work is relatively easy to find. Retired persons are now making comfortable livings in ways as diverse as starting a bee farm, raising capons for hotels, selling goats' milk, and running rodeos.

Living costs are up to you. Some of the southern California retirement towns are fairly lush, and to be "in the swim" one needs a fairly large, assured income. Further north, outward appearances are not so important.

For a minister, an interesting point about California is the number of churches. It is not uncommon for a town of 7,000 people to have twenty-five or thirty-five churches, all well-attended and prosperous. With this number of churches available, it is likely that there would be opportunities for a fair amount of supply work.

If none of these popular retirement areas appeals, there are always other places to investigate. Some folks realize, in retirement, their life-long dream of escaping to an island—and it doesn't have to be in the middle of the Pacific Ocean. The Virgin Islands and the Hawaiian Islands are gathering quite a harvest of retired couples. But although temperatures are pleasant and the pace is easy, living costs usually run high, and transportation is costly. It is virtually a necessity to survey the area first—since the move would represent so great a change in one's environment—and the cost of this alone could very well equal a year's retirement expenses in an area in the continental U.S.

Other folks go to the other extreme, and retire to the big city. They find in the metropolitan center the privacy they want, the tremendous cultural excitement, the great variety of clubs, activities, "things to do." They say that apartments can save you years of life over homes—with no gardening to do, no snow to remove, no walls to paint, no furnace to tend. They prefer the subway to driving a car. And they say that a careful shopper can get along on much less money than most people think big city life requires.

There is no one answer. As we said at the start of this chapter, where you live in your retirement years will ultimately depend on your individual preferences. And this material is designed solely to give you a bird's-eye view of the prospects that are available.

To concentrate and magnify this bird's-eye view, we suggest that you write for more detailed information to the areas or states that interest you. You will find in the appendix to this book ("Sources and Resources") a detailed bibliography which includes many volumes giving detailed descriptions of retirement sites.

But perhaps your best—and most up-to-date—sources of information will be state and city government offices and local Chambers of Commerce. A good gazetteer in your local library will give you geographical and climatological details; and the series of state guides published some years back under the auspices of the Federal Government (now known as the "American Guide Series") is packed with detailed information on every locality in the country.

Perhaps this material will seem less distant and more pertinent if we conclude with this survey printed in that excellent bi-weekly, *Monday Morning*, published in Philadelphia by The Presbyterian Church in the United States of America. Titled "Where Do Ministers Retire?", it was contributed by The Board of Pensions:

It seems to the Board of Pensions that ministers, their wives, and widows appear to retire everywhere and then do plenty of moving after that. Pension checks are sent to every state in the Union.

Each month 103 checks are sent to foreign countries. Surprisingly, not a single check is being sent to any country in continental Europe. There are 15 going to England, 2 to Ireland, but only 1 to Scotland. Some persons (6) chose Alaska for retirement while others select New Zealand (3), Hawaii (4), and places in South America, Mexico, Japan and India, but none are now in Africa.

Californians will be interested to know that 14 per cent—about one out of seven pension checks—go to persons in that state. Next comes Pennsylvania with 13 per cent of those receiving pensions. Then New York with 10 per cent, New Jersey with 5 per cent and Florida with 4 per cent (just a few more than the number now retired in Illinois).

However, there are 3.5 retired pensioners in Florida for every minister of our denomination who is actively serving a church in that state. In California there are a few more pensioners than active ministers—the ratio being 1.3 to 1. In Georgia the ratio is 3 to 1, Arkansas 2.7 to 1, Connecticut 2.2 to 1, Virginia 1.8 to 1, and then come North Carolina, South Carolina, Kentucky and Tennessee with a few more pensioners than active ministers.

As compared to ministers, the widows seem to prefer California, Colorado, Illinois, Tennessee, Maryland, District of Columbia, Ohio and Pennsylvania. The men seem to prefer Arizona, Nevada (which has no women pensioners), Oregon, Washington, Montana, Oklahoma, Connecticut, South Carolina, North Dakota, South Dakota, Florida. In the first group the ratio of women pensioners to men is much larger than normal. In the latter group, the minister-pensioners actually outnumber widows.

What states are "ideal" retirement locations? The Board asked this question of all women pensioners about three years ago (before smog became a common word) and discovered that, given complete freedom of choice, these widows thought they would like to live in the following locations: 16 per cent in California, 10 per cent in Pennsylvania, 7 per cent in Florida, 7 per cent in New York and 6 per cent in New Jersey. Those states which the women shunned were Nevada, Arizona, Utah, Vermont, New Hampshire, Maine, Rhode Island, Georgia, Mississippi, Louisiana. Most of the women would have preferred to live in small cities (54 per cent) while 24 per cent preferred a suburban area to a large city and the balance were equally divided between big cities (11 per cent) and rural or country areas (11 per cent). All of this leads one to conclude that ministers and their wives would be happy living anywhere in retirement if they had something interesting and important to do. Ministers as a whole seem to prefer the independent life in open spaces with possibilities for outdoor recreation, while widows prefer a location that is warm and comfortable, or near their family and old friends. These generalizations are based on statistical averages and there will be many who will take violent exception to any such conclusions. The fact is that, even at age 64, few persons really know where it would be best for them to retire!

We agree—"even at age 64," few persons have thought this vital retirement question through to a satisfactory, personal conclusion. Will you be one of those who fumbles and stumbles—or will you add joy and security to your years with the right decision, rightly-timed?

*Chapter Nine*

# YOUR HOME AFTER RETIREMENT

The question of where to live after retirement is a double-barreled one. Location is only half the problem. The other half concerns the kind of home it will be.

These are your choices: You can buy a house; build a house; rent a house or apartment; buy a trailer; move in with relatives; live in a denominational home for older persons; or live in a non-denominational home or community designed specifically for older persons.

When we apply the test of finances, the choice is narrowed for the average minister. Few have the funds to buy a house. Figures show that an infinitesimal percentage of mortgage loans are made to persons over sixty-five; there is simply not enough expectation of income to qualify such a person for a home loan.

The same hard facts militate against the minister building his own new home after retirement. Latest figures from the National Association of Real Estate Boards show the lowest average construction costs for a small, one-story frame house on a small lot to be $8,427. And this is in the lowest-cost area of the U.S.—Kentucky, Tennessee, Alabama, and Mississippi!

You can save money on a pre-cut, build-it-yourself home; but even this will run to about $4,000 before you are through if it's the average five-room, concrete-block house. And few ministers have had the opportunity to develop the handicraft skills necessary to undertake this construction chore, even if they do have sufficient capital to make the financial investment.

Moving in with relatives is unanimously discouraged by all experts in family relations. The chances of mutual happiness in a house where two (or, more likely, three) generations will be living side by side are quite slim. Privacy becomes a hit-or-miss proposition at best; independence of action exists only in theory; and even if you and your wife can make all the adjustments necessary to obtain peace and quiet, you would probably not be happy doing so.

No wonder, then, that it is a statistical fact that most people in the older age groups prefer to live in their own homes. L. S. Silk, writing in the *Journal of Gerontology*, says: "Over eighty percent of the urban and rural nonfarm families of people, sixty-five years of age and over, maintain independent households."

At the same time, however, another survey made by Wilber J. Cohen, in the *Annals of the American Academy of Political and Social Sciences*, reports that most people in the older age group are in low-income brackets and cannot afford today's building costs or rentals. Over 2,100,000 older persons, Mr. Cohen's survey showed, had annual incomes averaging under $500; another 2,300,000 persons had incomes between $500 and $999 a year; and 1,600,000 persons had an annual income of between $1,000 and $2,000.

The result is that most older persons—intent on preserving their independence but without the monetary means to do so properly—live in below-standard housing. A U.S. Housing and Home Finance Agency report declared that thirty-six percent of the homes in which older persons live *fall below acceptable standards for safety and sanitation*. In some larger cities, many older folk are forced to live in slum tenements. Here is the 1952 statement of the New York State Joint Legislative Committee on the Problems of the Aging:

"Our elderly live in houses or apartments constructed for younger people. They ramble around in big homes built for a period when they were raising a family. Or in crowded apartments booby-trapped by slippery floors, sliding rugs, dangerous equipment, death-trap bathtubs, poorly lighted rooms, or steps and stairways that take a toll of the heart. They live squeezed in with married children . . . in apartments likely to encourage conflict. You find them in the seedy rooming houses, in the slums, in the deteriorating neighborhoods, over a store, in the back flats, in a cubbyhole in a rooming house."

Renting a house or apartment has proved a stop-gap answer for many, although far too often the inexpensive quarters available also fall into the "minimum standard" category. And even at that they bite a huge chunk out of the budget. U.S. Labor Department figures show that the average yearly rent for a two- or three-room dwelling eats up slightly more than one-third of an elderly couple's total annual budget.

There is, however, a possible solution in the offing: the construction of special homes or communities for retired persons where they can live healthfully and happily at costs within their reach.

Unfortunately, this concept is still a new one. The number of such communities or homes is few, although their success is daily stimulating more activity. Another obstacle is the emotional reluctance of older people to relinquish even a shred of their independence, or to be identified in any way with what they inevitably think of as "the old folks' home."

This desire for continued independence in living arrangements is almost universal. Surveys everywhere show that older persons want to have their own homes even if they are sick, poor, or alone. In fact, they prefer sub-standard housing—in which they can still feel they are individuals—to above-standard housing in which they feel part of a mold.

But the forward-looking retired person should realize that the new approach—called by the experts "congregate living"—provides excellent housing without in any way intruding on privacy or independence.

"We are in the midst," reports a national news magazine, "of sweeping moves toward the construction of retirement communities all over the nation. Housing developments of the post-World War II period were for veterans desperately in need of shelter . . . Much of the building now going up from California to Florida will meet the needs of older people for a community of interests and independence."

The field is so new that developments are likely to outstrip the publication of this book. Public housing authorities as well as private builders are taking a hard look at population statistics which every year show millions more older persons in this nation; and they are jumping on the bandwagon with plans for houses, apartments—even entire villages—built specifically for the requirements of retired folk.

Kenneth L. Wilson, writing in "Lifetime Living" Magazine, said:

"An intriguing preview at Penney Farms, Florida, of how group-retirement housing can work has been attracting nationwide attention. This is the Memorial Home Community, a retirement home project comprising 110 acres planned for retired church people, YMCA workers and the like.

"The newest building in the community is the million-dollar quadrangle. No more institutional-looking than a garden apartment, it provides one hundred and twenty one-room apartments . . . For $3,500, an applicant buys an 'occupancy annuity,' entitling him to a home for as long as he needs it. When he dies, the apartment reverts to the Christian Herald Association, the owner, and is made available to someone else."

The Community is an outgrowth of the famous Penney Farms residence apartments designed for retired clergymen or missionaries and their wives. Heretofore when a husband or wife died, the surviving member had to leave the community so that it could operate at maximum usefulness. The new quadrangle with its one-room apartments will now accommodate these older single persons.

Penney Farms and the Memorial Home Community are only two of the scores of burgeoning opportunities for retired persons to take part in congregate living. All over the country—and especially in Florida and California—communities are being created to cater specifically to this group.

Most of them are planned communities complete from laundromat to shuffleboard court; many have retail stores on the premises; many encourage the persons who live there to indulge not only in hobbies but in part-time businesses as well. On-the-spot clinics, under the supervision of physicians and nurses, make instant and competent medical care available.

On entering most of these communities, the retired person *buys* his apartment or house. Prices vary, but most of them are within reach of the average retired person. With Social Security benefits now added to what ministers can expect from their pensions or annuity income, these communities are not beyond financial reach. One in Florida—Ormond by the Sea—charges $5,280 per living unit, but the down payment is only $690. The rest can be financed under an FHA Title I Loan if the buyer has an income of at least $140 a month. The mortgage can be amortized for a monthly payment of $31.85, which includes interest, repayment of principal, taxes and insurance.

Another community in Washington—Ryderwood Senior

Estates—sells its two-bedroom houses for $2,500, with a down payment of $200 and monthly payments of $20.00. The houses—part of an old "ghost" lumber town—have been refinished on the outside, but need fixing up on the inside. Residence here is restricted to persons having incomes of between $1,620 and $3,000 each year.

This income requirement is used in several other homes and communities. The feeling is that the restriction maintains morale in two ways: it guarantees that persons who can afford more expensive accommodations will not be granted favors; and it guarantees that there will be a community of interests among the people who live there.

Homes and communities for the retired persons are gradually growing more popular, chiefly because the stigma which used to be attached to "the old folks' home" has faded as modern communities for older persons improve. Now they are so tastefully planned and operated, and so ably encourage individual initiative in the form of social life and part-time work, that the aura of "incarceration" has been dispelled. Yet more than most men, ministers seem to have a resistance to such homes and communities. Because of this, many of the denominational homes maintained by church groups have not been as well patronized as one might think would be the case. For example, I was told of a quite lavish home in New York State built by the Congregational Church as a home for its retired ministers. It had to be abandoned after a few years simply because not enough retired ministers and their wives were interested in settling down there.

Most of the major denominations operate homes for their members, and some have homes specifically for their retired ministers. Virtually each requires an entrance fee of some kind; but some denominational homes give needy ministers a special grant to cover this sum if necessary. In a few cases, needy ministers living in a denominational home also receive a monthly stipend. Your own church is of course the best source for accurate and up-to-date information about denominational homes which may be available for your retirement years.

Here are some examples of denominational homes as described in *Housing the Aging,* a report on a seminar on the subject edited by Professor Wilma Donahue and published by the University of Michigan Press:

> Pilgrim Place, in Claremont, California sponsored by the Congregational Church . . . demonstrates how a community for retired persons can be made an integral part of a city . . . The village is restricted to retired missionaries, ministers and other Christian workers, although they need not be of Congregational persuasion. . . . The community consists of residence halls with small apartments for single men and women, and of small homes which are either privately owned by their residents or owned by Pilgrim Place.
>
> Because Pilgrim Place is a non-profit organization, rental charges are kept between one-half and two-thirds of commensurate commercial values . . . An infirmary and nursing home has recently been built on the grounds. . . . Houses vary in style and the village seems no different than any city street. The naturalness of the setting, the absence of institutionalized program features, and the freedom of the residents to live independently make this project one of great significance.
>
> At Charlotte, North Carolina, the Methodist Home for the Aging has a large well-equipped central building. In it are common dining rooms, an excellent infirmary, sitting rooms, recreation halls and theater, chapel, occupational therapy shops, and store. The building houses approximately one hundred and fifty people in individual rooms complete with private baths. Nearby

is a row-house development in which there are one- and two-bedroom units. The residents of these apartments may prepare breakfast and supper in their kitchens but are expected to take their noon meals in the main dining room . . . Great attention is given to the planning of social and educational programs which will meet the needs of the residents for participation in interesting activities . . .

In Detroit, Michigan, a new program is underway, sponsored by the Presbyterian Church. After making a decision that they should develop a plan which would help solve the housing needs of the able-bodied, the frail, and the sick, and after a careful study of the facts and trends in the aging population, the planning group produced a blueprint for Presbyterian Village. This community is to be located on a plot of about thirty-five acres which lies outside the city limits but which is in the midst of a new suburban shopping center and community.

For the latest data and information about congregate living communities and non-denominational or denominational homes, you can write either to the Chamber of Commerce of a community; or to the appropriate State Department of Development. For general information, write to Investors Diversified Services, Inc., Minneapolis, Minnesota, a private research group devoting much of its energies to the problems of housing for older persons. If they cannot immediately answer your specific questions, these groups will at least be in a position to refer you to other sources.

The house you live in can have a good deal to do with your health. Above all else, if your house is clean, bright, comfortable and cheerful, *you* will be cheerful. If your house is poorly-lighted, difficult to keep clean, and generally not suited to your needs and wants, it will have a depressing effect.

Only recently have housing specialists given thought to the *specific* housing requirements of older men and women. Indicative of this long-overdue awakening is an order issued not too long ago by the New York State Division of Housing: any low-rent housing development expecting to get state financial aid in its construction must set aside and specially design for elderly persons at least five per cent of its available apartments.

What does the N.Y. State Department of Housing consider "special features for elderly persons?" Here are some of the items: non-slip floor for bathrooms; square bathtubs with seats in the tubs and handgrips in the walls to help an older person get in and out of the tub; shower stalls with seats and hand grips; no thresholds between doors (to cut down on tripping accidents); electric stoves instead of gas stoves; shelves and storage cabinets built at lower, easier-to-reach levels; mechanically-operated casement windows. The apartments are also to be on the sunniest side of the building and to have more heat available.

You'll notice that virtually all of these "special features" are concerned with the preservation of health and the elimination of accidents—proof that the kind of place you live in has a great deal to do with how long and how healthily you'll live. Choose it as carefully as you can!

*Chapter Ten*

# TRAVEL AFTER RETIREMENT

For the first time in your life, you'll have unlimited time for travel. Yes, the first day of your retirement will be that magic "someday" when you are going to do all the things the busy schedule of your life has previously prevented. And travel—for most of us—leads the list.

Travel takes money, of course, whether it be an around-the-world-trip by air, or a bouncing ride by bus to the state park in the next county. But it need not take as much money as you think.

The boom in travel has given birth to a fabulous variety of special travel plans and arrangements; and each one somehow succeeds in giving the traveler more than his money's worth.

"This change," travel expert Mary Parker writes, "has deliberately been brought about by transportation companies and resort areas. They have demonstrated that . . . travel is about the most economical thing anyone can do."

From the viewpoint of savings, the most important of these special approaches calls for off-season travel. More people now go to Florida in the summertime, for example, than do in the wintertime. And the rates at the glamorous hotels, the name restaurants—even at the roadside hamburger stands—are anywhere from twenty-five percent to fifty percent cheaper than at the height of the so-called "season."

While winter resorts have been changing into summer resorts, summer resorts have been transforming themselves into winter playlands. New England, Eastern Canada and other vacation retreats used to compress their whole season into the summer months; now they encourage a steady stream of visitors throughout the year.

Europe, which used to see American tourists only between Memorial Day and Labor Day, now entertains them all year round. We're urged by private and government tourist bureaus alike to "make our visits after the height of the holiday rush."

This is easier said than done by most Americans—but it goes hand-in-glove with the needs and desires of the retired minister.

He saves money on transportation; both air and ship lines usually offer special rates between October and April. (Some go a step further with so-called "family fares"—still lower rates for a wife when she travels with her husband.)

And he saves money on hotel accommodations—perhaps as much as thirty to forty percent on both room and food.

He is accorded better and more gracious attention during his travels. Everyone from porters at the railroad stations to headwaiters at hotel dining-rooms is less harried, less rushed and crushed by pressing chores. People have time to chat with you, explain things to you, make you feel truly welcome and wanted.

Most important, perhaps, is the fact that the off-season traveler really gets to know the people who live in the area he is visiting. The French say that "only Americans and Englishmen live in Paris during the summer"—and there is considerable truth in this, for when the tourists move in on a city like an army, the natives usually move out. One minister summed this up for me with a little anecdote about his experiences in Stockholm. "The first time I went there," he said, "it was at the height of the tourist influx. When I stopped someone on the street to ask directions, the answer most often was: 'I'm sorry, but I'm a stranger here myself.' When I was next in Stockholm, however, it was about as off-season as could be. And when I asked a passerby for directions, I would not only get them—but I'd hear a delightful discourse as well on the buildings I would pass on this street, the monument I would see on that street, and the restaurants which might be in between. A moment or two later this same person would ask me if I by any chance knew his cousin in Chicago (I'm from Dallas myself!)—and all the while my wife would be receiving a short course on cooking delicate little Swedish meat-balls!"

Finally—the more time you have on a visit, the less money you need! If this seems like a paradox, let me explain with one illustration. There are several ways to get from Paris to Rome. If you have only two weeks on the Continent and want to visit both cities, you'll have to fly from France to Italy . . . the trip will take only a few hours, but will cost at least one hundred dollars for two people. If you take a more time-consuming form of transportation —a railroad—you'll travel by rail for some two days for the round-trip, but you'll save more than half in fares. And if you are really relaxed about time, and go by bus—you'll save even more, and have a breathtaking, unforgettable tour of two countries as well.

You'll even find that food and lodging cost less when your time is your own. You'll "discover" little neighborhood restaurants rarely entered by tourists; the food will be magnificent, and the charges small. You'll be invited to visit private homes. You'll have time to discover which are the least expensive areas of a city, and which the most.

Most important—you'll have the leisure and wisdom to savor new scenes, and wring learning from new experiences.

One minister and his wife told me that a trip they made after retirement to the Bible lands gave them deep, new insights into the stories of the Old and New Testaments.

What do you want out of travel? The chance to see how other people live? An opportunity to view magnificent treasures of art? Perhaps a visit to the city from which your forebears came? Do you want to continue important research in a field in which you've been working and writing? Is this to be a cruise in the nature of a "reward and present" to your wife? Or is the journey to be made for reasons of health?

The reasons for travel are so many and diverse—and the places to which one can go so unlimited—that it would be impossible to cover the endless range in one book. Instead, let us survey some general points which you should remember when you begin to think in practical terms about travel after retirement.

*1.* Rates are constantly in flux. The "budget" which Minister A and his wife found so workable in 1954 will be of little or no value to Minister B in 1956. You *can* get reliable, up-to-date figures on travel costs, however, from any local travel agent; and this service doesn't cost you a penny, not even if you book yourself for a round-the-world tour covering thirty cities. Travel agents make their money on commissions paid them by transportation lines and hotels. If you want information which goes deeper into living-costs than fares and hotel rates, you can get them too without charge by writing to your U. S. consulates, or to the embassies of foreign countries. Incidentally, many lines now have attractive "installment plans" which permit you to pay for a trip after you make it.

2. Plan as much ahead as possible . . . and perhaps you'll be able to find ways to earn money while traveling. One minister in New York, for example, makes arrangements to write articles for his denominational publication

from overseas. These stories do not pay for his trip by any means—but they do produce extra dollars for extra enjoyment; he buys books and gifts abroad which he otherwise could not afford. Another friend—not a minister—places small advertisements in the "Personals" section of his newspaper when he is contemplating a trip, in which he offers to carry out a variety of personal commissions for people while abroad. Such commissions may range from the delivery of a family heirloom to the purchase of a specific piece of machinery. Once he was simply asked to visit the resting-place of a G.I. who lost his life in Normandy, and make certain that the grave was in good condition; and for this humanitarian task he was paid travel expenses from England to France.

*3.* Investigate the "bargain" methods of travel. For example, among the ships which ply their way across the Atlantic and the Pacific are one-class liners, freighters, and cargo-passenger ships. These vessels have certain tremendous advantages for the budget-conscious passenger. There is no need to be "dressy." The cabins are fewer, and are usually all "outside cabins"—more comfortable, larger, airier. Because there are fewer passengers, your opportunity to make friends is enhanced. The trip is a leisurely one; stops are sometimes made at exciting port cities you might otherwise miss. And rates are dramatically smaller than on the fancy-and-frilly ocean-liners—often fifty or sixty percent less!

Don't be leery of freighters and cargo-passenger ships: the food served on them is uniformly good, the crews are friendly and helpful (and not nearly so tip-conscious!), and the accommodations are clean. And since these ships are usually heavily-loaded, they tend to ride "lower" in the water than the big liners, which makes for a smoother ride. Incidentally, don't let any tendency to motion-sickness deter you from travel. Dramamine, now sold over-the-counter without a prescription, is effective against motion sickness for several hours. And a new drug, Bonamine, promises effective protection for as much as twenty-four hours. Bonamine is now sold by prescription only, but will probably soon be available over-the-counter.

*4.* Railroad companies are now making many financial concessions to potential passengers. Weekday and off-season travel is often charged for at lower rates; wives travelling with their husbands pay only half-fare on some lines; stop-over and re-routing privileges are growing more elastic; many trains are adding low-cost cafeteria-cars for passengers who either cannot afford or do not like the more expensive dining cars.

*5.* Bus travel is becoming more comfortable and convenient. Many bus lines are copying rail lines, offering special rates for family travel, expanding their stop-over privileges. Greyhound has recently introduced its new super-bus, the Scenicruiser, a double-decked giant with reclining seats, a washroom in the bus, specially-wide windows, and a host of other extras. Any bus line will be glad to plan a tour itinerary for you, and will make hotel reservations for you at stopovers en route.

*6.* Automobile travel is also being made more pleasant by the mushrooming of elaborate motels and tourist courts, by the growth of the "drive-in lobby" for hotels (which permits the auto traveler to register right from his car), and by the improved network of superhighways which make driving quicker and less nerve-wracking.

The big objection to auto travel—the traffic-packed highway—is no handicap to the retired person. He can take his trip during weekdays, or off-season months. Your best bet for help in auto travel is the American Automobile Association.

*7.* If you go overseas, investigate the opportunity to see more of the land and meet more of the people by traveling by rail, bus or even private car. Most foreign countries have special rates and even elaborate tours available to the American visitor who wants to move about by rail. And several private companies operate extremely good bus-tours on the same basis.

The idea of touring Europe in your own car is not so lavish or spendthrift as it may seem. You can either rent a car when you arrive overseas; or you can buy one under the "guaranteed repurchase" plan now in effect. Under this plan, the seller contracts to buy the car back from you before you leave for home, repurchasing it at a price slightly less than the sum you paid for it. You are, in effect, *renting* the car. The purchase plan merely saves you some fees and red tape. The small European cars are easy to handle and get tremendous mileage (up to forty-five miles) out of a gallon of gas. Renting one can save further money for you by enabling you to stop over in less-expensive small towns, at *pensions* and in out-of-the-way hotels.

*8.* Health requirements are simple. You will probably need a smallpox vaccination, since the U.S. Government will not let you back in the country unless you have been vaccinated within the last three years.

You should consult your doctor before traveling to foreign countries. He will advise you on general health problems (Should I drink the water? Should I eat fresh fruit and vegetables?) and will also make suggestions as to what other shots, if any (such as those for typhus and typhoid) he may think desirable.

*9.* Don't let the paperwork of travel throw you. You must have a U.S. passport if you leave the country (except when you go to Mexico, Canada and most Caribbean islands). But few European nations still require a U.S. citizen to get a visa. Any travel agent or travel company will be glad to give you a list of the required papers for any country you may be thinking of visiting.

And if you want to avoid the problems attendant on changing U.S. dollars into foreign currency, you can simply take traveler's checks with you, cashing them when and as you need them. You may lose a lire or a franc or two on the transaction, but the convenience and safety gained will far outweigh that loss.

If handling passports and money and baggage—if the thought of customs and immigration inspectors—are really enough to dissuade you from overseas travel, investigate the "package tour" or the "group travel" plan. The tour host or director generally handles all this routine for his group, relieving you of all problems and worries. Package tours are also among the most economical of travel devices. For one thing, costs are generally all-inclusive—meals, tips, fees, and so forth. Thus you know before you start exactly what your total expenses will be. But be sure to read the fine print, or to consult a reputable travel agent so that you do not get stuck with hidden "extras."

*10.* You might give a thought—now that you are retired and have all the time in the world—to living abroad for a while. Many sections of the world offer astounding bargains: magnificent villas for $90 a month on the French Riviera; fully-furnished and staffed houses in South American garden-spots for at little as $60 a month. If you shop around you can find truly wonderful places to live where your total expenses may not exceed $2,000 a year.

However, there is one big drawback to this glamorous picture: You are likely to be lonely. Unless you are exceptionally gregarious and adaptable, you will be a stranger in a strange land, and your acquaintanceships will seldom ripen into the kind of true friendships you can have at home.

*11.* Did you know you could take a trip to Europe absolutely free—an *all-expenses-paid* trip including such luxuries as a car and chauffeur at your disposal while you tour for some five weeks through seven foreign countries?

Of course there is a "catch" to this—otherwise the airlines and ship companies would soon be on the way to bankruptcy. But it is a "catch" that is not too difficult to cope with. As a matter of fact, hundreds of people have already made their trip to Europe just this way.

Here is how writer Mort Weisinger explains it in his book, "1001 Valuable Things You Can Get Free," published by Grosset & Dunlap at $1.00, and by Bantam Books in a paper-bound edition at only twenty-five cents. It is, incidentally, an excellent reference book for a retired man to read:

> To get this free European round trip, you must get five friends to take the trip with you. If you can organize them into going together as one party, you can go along with them, absolutely free, with all your expenses paid. Your free trip is sort of an agent's commission.
>
> Here are the three tours which are offered in this unique give-away. If you get five people to go on any of the following tours, you can go "on the house." The house in this particular situation is the reputable Washington, D. C. travel bureau—the Lanseair Travel Service, Inc.
>
> Tour 1. England, France, Italy, Austria, Switzerland, Germany, Luxembourg. Time: 32 days. Cost (including all travel, hotels, meals): $1,394.
>
> Tour 2. Scotland, England, Belgium, Holland, Germany, Switzerland, Austria, Italy, France. Time: 34 days. Cost: $1,419.
>
> Tour 3. France, Italy, Austria, Switzerland, Germany, Holland, Belgium. Time: 30 days. Cost: $1,389.
>
> Pick the tour you want and then get in touch with the Lanseair Travel Service, Inc., DuPont Circle Bldg., Washington 6, D. C. Lanseair will send you copies of the detailed itinerary describing the trip and free bonus plan.
>
> Start organizing your own party (five others besides yourself) and let Lanseair know when you want to leave N.Y. so reservations can be made.

Each person's reservation (except, of course, the organizer's) should include a deposit of $200. Should any member of the party decide to bow out, or if the trip is canceled, this deposit is refundable."

*12.* Travel by trailer has become so popular in recent years, and so economical, that it is virtually as much a way of life for retired persons as it is a means of transportation. Trailerites used to be considered somewhat akin to gypsies. They lived in small box-like contraptions which careened after their cars; and they set up housekeeping on the sides of roads.

But increasing numbers of substantial people saw the advantages of trailer life. Over 2,000,000 people, in fact, now travel and live in them. And with each day the trailer industry continues to skyrocket to even greater popularity.

Why? Well, first of all—better trailers are being built. Today you can buy a trailer which ranges anywhere from sixteen feet to sixty feet in length; prices for them range from $1,500 to $7,500. And thousands of second-hand trailers—in excellent condition—can be picked up for as little as $500 for the smaller ones to about $3,000 for the big ones.

The deluxe models come equipped with built-in toilets and showers, refrigerators, butane-gas stoves, electric outlets—even wall-to-wall carpeting, portable phones and television sets! They are simple to hitch on and off the car, easy to haul and simple to park.

Second, major credit concerns have developed long-term financing for trailer purchases. Admittedly the original investment is high, but the upkeep is virtually negligible.

Third—and perhaps most important—trailer parks have zoomed to popularity. These are places where trailerites can set up homes alongside like-minded people, and such sites have grown from mere weedy lots to beautifully-designed, elaborate layouts in recent years. Some of them offer services which range from breakfast in bed to a private boat- or fishing-dock.

A trailer park in Melbourne, Florida, is now serving as an "experimental laboratory" for trailer life. Here they are gathering facts on trailerites' requirements, expenses, desires. The information gained will help to set standards for future park planning. Meanwhile, *The Trailer Park Guide,* a publication of the Trailer Coach Manufacturing Association, can serve you as a guide to current acceptable trailer parks.

Trailerites are rhapsodic in their descriptions of the life they lead. Some are content to move but once a year—from their summer home in a Northern or Western trailer-park to their winter home in a Florida camp. Others are more footloose, and pull up stakes every few weeks, following the sun and the seasons and their own inclinations. Trailerites praise the fellowship of the road, too.

But isn't this expensive? Well, trailer families say that apart from the cost of the trailer itself, life couldn't be cheaper.

Here are their standing costs: about fifty cents a week for butane gas, fifty cents a week for electricity, about one-third more cost for gasoline than when driving a car alone; and trailer-park rent. This can run from about ten dollars a month in a plain and simple establishment to as much as forty or fifty dollars a month in a luxurious one. There are scarcely any maintenance costs for the trailer; food costs run the same as if you lived in a house; there are no taxes to pay, no handymen to pay, no heating bills to pay, no repairs to make. Here is a direct quote from one trailer expert:

> I dare say that a retired couple, once their trailer investment is made (and remember that the purchase price includes everything—house, furniture, equip-

ment, even window draperies) can easily live a whole year on less than $500, exclusive of food and personal expenditures. It *can* be done for $300—and in the pleasantest spots in the nation.

Increasing numbers of retired ministers are finding trailer travel and trailer living the best solution to their problems. Some ministers have said that the freedom of movement the trailer gives them has made it possible for them to gain more pulpit supply work than they otherwise would, for it brings them into areas where many near-by small towns often lack the services of a minister.

Here, for instance, is what the Reverend C. E. Burkhart of Madison, Minnesota, said in a letter to one trailer manufacturing company, the Rollohome Corporation in Marshfield, Wisconsin:

> We choose to live in a mobile home during retirement because we know it's a way of life that makes a fitting conclusion to a lifetime devoted to the ministry.
>
> In the first place, just owning our own mobile home will be a thrill we've never been able to have. The average minister spends his life in parsonages or manses owned by the churches he serves. Some congregations are more lenient than others in giving the minister leeway as to decorating and permanent furnishings, but we've never been able to have the thrill of saying, "This is ours to do with as we please!"
>
> The modern mobile home offers conveniences and comforts that we haven't always had. It offers a completion of living necessities and in a compact space that cuts down maintenance labor and leaves time for leisure pursuits. There is room enough for hobbies and space for an adequate library so that I won't feel that I've left behind everything connected with my work. The

adequate kitchen facilities will make housekeeping a real joy to my wife.

The very mobility of the mobile home is in itself its greatest asset. Retirement brings with it a freedom from schedule and from appointments so when the urge strikes us to move on, we can do it. We can follow the seasons as we like. If we choose to spend a summer at the lake, nothing will stop us. If we want to avoid the rigors of a northern winter, we can go south; but we know that if we stay in the north we'll be cozier in our mobile home than we ever were in large drafty houses.

Another thing we'll especially enjoy will be the independence of having our own home. Should illness strike either of us, we can park near our children where we can have care without giving up previous independence. If one of us should be left alone the remaining one can still be sure of an independent home filled with happy memories. We can be near our children without any invasion of privacy for any of us.

The economy of a mobile home enters especially into our picture since, like all ministers, our savings are small. *No other mode of living offers as many luxuries for so little money.* Our entire savings doesn't have to go toward buying a home and furniture.

But wherever you go and however you get there, travel itself is the important thing. Even going a little way down the road enables you to see your own backyard in a new perspective.

For the retired person, travel is almost a necessity. With its chores simplified and its costs brought down to within the reach of virtually everyone, travel is vital to an understanding of the world we live in, and to an understanding of ourselves.

And travel is the most effective way of keeping young in mind, heart, and in the spirit.

*Chapter Eleven*

# YOUR HEALTH AFTER RETIREMENT

Franklin Roosevelt made many speeches, and left many phrases indelibly stamped on American history. Perhaps the one which will be longest remembered is his simple declaration: "We have nothing to fear but fear itself."

This is especially true of the older person. We know it—yet all of us, no matter how strong our spiritual faith, are brought up short at one time or another by the idea of aging. For the concept of "oldness" perversely enough brings to mind not the assets of that state, but all its real and fancied liabilities. Not the joys, but the fears.

Chief among these fears is the prospect of poor health. And yet if we could only cut through the preconceived notion that old age is automatically a period of poor health, the truth would be apparent. And the truth is that modern medical and nutritional science have freed older persons from many of the threats of illness.

High blood pressure and occluded coronaries, failing sight and arthritic aches do *not* automatically descend on one at a certain birthday. Aging is a phase of life's eternal cycle; it may bring with it certain reductions in strength and endurance, and perhaps a few restrictions, but it is not in itself a disease.

"Poor health and old age do not have to go together," one prominent medical expert has said. "If you think of your body as a chain made up of many links, links which represent the various organs, you can learn how to help maintain your health despite your increased age.

"When the body is young, for example, each link is strong enough to take up more than its share of strain and work. As the body matures, the links weaken gradually. Some weaken sooner than others. And if a weak link is subjected to too much stress—such as disease or overwork—it may snap, resulting in illness. But although you cannot halt the inevitable aging of your body, you can do much to cut down the extra strains the various links receive."

There is no longer any age at which a person is "old." In the days of Greece's glory and Rome's grandeur, most men and women died before they were thirty or forty; as science advanced, so did man's life expectancy. A child born today has a slightly longer life expectancy than the three score and ten years the Bible grants him. On the other hand, of course, he is still nowhere near the one hundred and twenty years which the Lord said his days shall be (Genesis, 6:3). But even that mark will more than likely be surpassed in succeeding generations. Man should, the experts say, have a life span of one hundred and fifty years—or about seven times his age at maturity, just as all other mammals do.

Data released by the U.S. National Office of Vital Statistics yields the life expectancy shown in the table on p. 150. The most important lesson these figures teach is that your year of retirement can be the start of *many years of living for you*—years which should be as healthy as you can make them.

Is there anything you can do to prolong your life span? Indeed, yes. For one thing, you can take care of your body by observing good health habits. Second, you can make sure your environment (and this means your home, your work or hobby, the climate you live in) is as beneficial as possible. Third, you can adjust reasonably to the emotional and psychological pressures of retirement. Fourth, you can bend your efforts to constructive activity and positive thinking. Here are the statistics:

| | YEARS REMAINING | |
|---|---|---|
| *At Age* | *For Men* | *For Women* |
| 45 | 26.5 | 30.5 |
| 50 | 22.4 | 26.2 |
| 55 | 18.8 | 22.0 |
| 60 | 15.4 | 18.1 |
| 65 | 12.4 | 14.4 |
| 70 | 9.8 | 11.2 |
| 75 | 7.5 | 8.3 |
| 80 | 5.4 | 5.8 |
| 85 | 3.6 | 3.7 |

The Metropolitan Life Insurance Company, which for years has done outstanding work in the field of health, recommends above all periodic medical examinations if you want a healthy old age.

"During these examinations," it says in its pamphlet, *Your Future and You,* "your doctor will search for any evidences of disease. . . . Many of the chronic or degenerative diseases develop without symptoms early in their course because the reserve strength of the organs can—for a while—make up for the damage being done. If the disease is not discovered until warning symptoms are sent out—until you no longer feel fine—the body's power of self-repair may be considerably diminished."

What are the chronic diseases which silently grow during the middle and later years? Cancer, heart and blood vessel ailments, diabetes, nephritis. The symptoms of some are minor: a stiffness in a joint, a persistent blemish on the skin. But they cannot and should not be airily dismissed with a "Well, what can I expect when I get old?" The older you get, the more significance these minor symptoms can have, and the more important it becomes for you to have regular and thorough physical examinations.

A second health habit recommended by every expert is that you eat the proper amount of the proper foods each day. Too many older people fall into the practice of eating "pick-up" meals. They use as excuses the fact that they "have no appetite" or "don't want to shop and cook for myself." Some overeat to "keep up strength." Others undereat because they worry about their "digestion." Still others embark on food fads and weird diets.

A recent trend in food packaging can eventually become a major aid to the older person who does want to eat well and properly, hopes to keep his weight at the right level, and yet does not wish to bother much with shopping and food preparation. It's the development of special canned foods for older people.

Doctors have known for many years that older people require fewer calories, less salt, and more minerals and protein in their diet. Yet except for a few hard-to-find and expensive specialty lines, there was no food designed especially for them—as there is, for example, for babies or diabetics, who also have specific food needs.

But only a few months ago one major food company, H. J. Heinz, started test-marketing its new "Senior Foods." These are one-serving, eight-and-one-half-ounce cans which sell for about a quarter each. The first "senior foods" available are beef, lamb and chicken stews; and if the natural reluctance of an older person to admit he is a "senior" can be overcome, the producer plans to offer vegetables, fruits and custard desserts next.

It is true that as you mature you do not need to eat as *much* food as in your more physically energetic years. But you should still eat the right *kinds* of food. Nutritionists say that each day's food intake should include these elements:

Green and yellow leafy vegetables—at least one serving.

Tomatoes and citrus fruits, or raw cabbage—at least one serving.

Potatoes, and other vegetables and fruits—at least two servings.

Milk and milk products—at least a pint.

Meat, fish or poultry—at least one serving.

Eggs—five a week.

Bread and cereal—either one or both at each meal.

Butter, margarine or other fats—at least two tablespoonsful.

You should not gain weight, nor continue in an overweight condition. Research has shown that the older person is best off if he stays within the weight range which would have been normal for his body-build at the age of twenty-five. Opposite is a chart of desirable weights according to your height and build, based on actuarial studies of hundreds of thousands of men and women. Study it and make good use of it.

Use common sense not only in nutrition, but in all the day-to-day activities of your life. Not everyone needs the same amount of sleep. Some folks require more exercise than others. Some people can work longer than others without feeling tired. With your own doctor, during one of your periodic physical examinations, you'll be able to arrive at a set of good health habits which meet your particular needs. Then stick to them to the best of your ability!

And don't overlook those hazards to health which come from accidents! One-third of all accidental deaths occur

## MEN

*Weight in Pounds According to Frame (as Ordinarily Dressed)*

| HEIGHT (with shoes on) 1-inch heels Feet | Inches | SMALL FRAME | MEDIUM FRAME | LARGE FRAME |
|---|---|---|---|---|
| 5 | 2 | 116–125 | 124–133 | 131–142 |
| 5 | 3 | 119–128 | 127–136 | 133–144 |
| 5 | 4 | 122–132 | 130–140 | 137–149 |
| 5 | 5 | 126–136 | 134–144 | 141–153 |
| 5 | 6 | 129–139 | 137–147 | 145–157 |
| 5 | 7 | 133–143 | 141–151 | 149–162 |
| 5 | 8 | 136–147 | 145–156 | 153–166 |
| 5 | 9 | 140–151 | 149–160 | 157–170 |
| 5 | 10 | 144–155 | 153–164 | 161–175 |
| 5 | 11 | 148–159 | 157–168 | 165–180 |
| 6 | 0 | 152–164 | 161–173 | 169–185 |
| 6 | 1 | 157–169 | 166–178 | 174–190 |
| 6 | 2 | 163–175 | 171–184 | 179–196 |
| 6 | 3 | 168–180 | 176–189 | 184–202 |

## WOMEN

| HEIGHT (with shoes on) 2-inch heels Feet | Inches | SMALL FRAME | MEDIUM FRAME | LARGE FRAME |
|---|---|---|---|---|
| 4 | 11 | 104–111 | 110–118 | 117–127 |
| 5 | 0 | 105–113 | 112–120 | 119–129 |
| 5 | 1 | 107–115 | 114–122 | 121–131 |
| 5 | 2 | 110–118 | 117–125 | 124–135 |
| 5 | 3 | 113–121 | 120–128 | 127–138 |
| 5 | 4 | 116–125 | 124–132 | 131–142 |
| 5 | 5 | 119–128 | 127–135 | 133–145 |
| 5 | 6 | 123–132 | 130–140 | 138–150 |
| 5 | 7 | 126–136 | 134–144 | 142–154 |
| 5 | 8 | 129–139 | 137–147 | 145–158 |
| 5 | 9 | 133–143 | 141–151 | 149–162 |
| 5 | 10 | 136–147 | 145–155 | 152–166 |
| 5 | 11 | 139–150 | 148–158 | 155–169 |

with people over sixty-five. And to make this all the more lamentable, a lot of accidents aren't really accidents. They occur because a person is either careless or (because of some emotional problem) is "accident-prone."

You can easily develop a sensible awareness of the hazards which occur with regularity in your environment. Make it a habit to allow yourself more time to cross the street as you grow older; if you drive, be even more careful than you have always been; check the electric outlets and the gas knobs of your stove regularly. There's nothing to be ashamed of in doing these things; it's not an admission of senility, nor evidence that you are ripe for the old folks' home. It's merely a sensible precaution with your most precious possession—your retirement years.

What about mental health? Although most people never voice their worries on this score, the fact is that aging people are just as much concerned over "going into a second childhood" as they are about physical afflictions.

Well, do your brains wear out from overwork or long usage? Of course they don't!

In the relatively few cases of senile dementia (the technical term for "second childhood") which do occur, there is actual physical deterioration of the brain cells. But it's caused by disease, not by overwork! Physicians say that the healthier you are now, the greater are the chances you'll continue to be alert for the rest of your life.

And if illness—physical or mental—does occur, American medicine is in a better position than ever before to attack it and conquer it. Increased research and the use of new drugs are successfully beating back the onslaughts of illness. The antibiotics—the "wonder drugs"—have licked whole classes of illness. Pneumonia, which not too long ago was virtually a sentence of death for an older person, is now generally no more dangerous than a very bad cold. Infectious diseases have largely been conquered.

Other drugs—relaxants—are opening the door to effective treatment of blood vessel diseases: hardening of the arteries, for instance, and high blood pressure. Heart disease is not the killer we once thought it was, and this is true despite the fact that it is still the official cause of more than fifty percent of all deaths in the U.S. (But that's because so many people are *not* dying from other diseases which used to be killers!) Eighty-five percent of those who survive a first coronary attack recover well enough to carry on a normal life; they can avoid a second attack if they take the proper precautions.

Incidentally, it's estimated that three out of every four persons who think they have heart disease *don't have it!*

Right behind actual heart and blood-vessel ailments as a leading cause of death is cancer, perhaps the most fearsome illness known to man. Yet, *worry* about cancer may be just as killing as cancer itself; some experts in the field of cancer prevention have recently asked themselves whether the emphasis on cancer detection and prevention is, by focusing so much thought on cancer, actually contributing to its incidence.

Even against this scourge, however, medical science is making steady progress. Better and prompter diagnosis, plus improved surgical and radiological therapy, is affecting many more cures than ever before. Only one person in seven dies of cancer. And even these odds will be more heavily weighted in your favor if you keep your semi-annual date with your doctor for a physical checkup.

The condition possibly most closely related to your day-to-day health is the climate. Although there is no such thing as a "perfect" climate anywhere, one need not be a climatologist or physician to know that warm sun, dry air and a steady barometer are more conducive to pleasant and relaxed living than cold winds, soggy humidity and stormy weather. A top expert on climate and its relation to health has written that the seasonal changes between hot summers and cold winters in the northern sections of the U.S. are a physical strain on older people, who do not adjust with resiliency to wide-swinging weather extremes.

But when you try to find a climate without one or another drawback for the retired person, you have—let's admit it—some trouble. The South is fine in winter, but hot in summer. The coast may be breeze-cooled, but it's likely to be dampish. The crisp air of high altitudes may be too stimulating.

The ideal solution is to follow the sun as the seasons change; this however calls for more than one home, or else heavy transportation expenses, and is generally too costly for the average retired minister even to consider.

The next logical solution is to consider climate as one of the most important factors when deciding where to make your permanent post-retirement home. For your convenience, the basic climatic data for various cities has been included in this book.

Of course not everyone reacts the same way to the same climate. Mr. Jones may be delighted with the balmy breezes of Florida, while Mr. Smith may hate them. Suitable climate depends not only on what nature provides, but on the health, habits and temperament of the person involved.

Specific ailments are also affected by climate. Rigorous weather requiring constant bodily adjustments to climate is a strain on heart ailment sufferers, as well as on those who have high blood pressure, nephritis, digestive disorders, and diabetes. The best areas for these conditions are Southern Florida, California and the Southwest.

Respiratory ailments are helped most by a dry climate, and by an atmosphere which remains unpolluted by dust, smog and pollens. Suggested regions include southwestern Texas (near El Paso), Southern New Mexico and Arizona, and Southern California (except, in the latter area, on the coastal fringe, where inshore winds carry large amounts of moisture).

The same areas are kind to sufferers from rheumatic and arthritic ailments, not only because of the absence of cold and dampness, but because sudden changes of temperature and barometric pressure are similarly absent.

The Southwest is pollen-free, but if you are generally an "allergic" type, it would be a good idea to have your doctor definitely identify the specific causes of your allergy. You might well be jumping out of the frying pan into the fire!

Two other factors are sun and altitude. There is still some discussion as to whether too much exposure to the sun causes or speeds skin cancer. You will get more sun not only if you move South, but if you move to high-altitude country. Altitude is also accompanied by higher winds, lower temperatures and air pressure. The rate of metabolism and of breathing is speeded up, and can produce an effect of nervous tension and excitability.

A last word of caution: If you suffer from a specific ailment and plan to move to a new climate, discuss your plans first with your doctor. Make sure the new climate will not affect you adversely. Never make a drastic change to another climate without getting medical advice first.

*Chapter Twelve*

# YOUR MARRIAGE AND RETIREMENT

In the press of ministerial activities, a minister may sometimes forget that he has a wife.

One woman, married to a clergyman for twenty-five years, told me: "When things were really hectic and busy, I'm sure John used to consider me not as his wife, but as an assistant pastor in charge of all the things he didn't have time to do himself."

This is probably more faithful to the fact than many ministers would care to admit. Too often a wife simply becomes someone who keeps house, calls the children out of the study, plays the piano for the choral group, and bakes cakes for the annual Ladies Circle picnic. Her function as helpmate, soulmate, friend and companion is lost in a jungle of countless activities.

Then—the minister retires. Then—there are no more ladies' groups to be coddled, no more singers to be kept "on pitch"; the children who used to interrupt when sermons were being created are now grown up and gone away.

Now—it is just you and your wife, trying to pick up the threads of the years.

You will find that retirement brings a new meaning to the sunset years of your marriage. Although at first it may seem to your wife that she is no longer needed and that "there is nothing for her to do," the truth is that you will soon realize that you are "partners" more than ever before.

You and your wife have many advantages over most couples who enter the retirement years together. The average couple have been apart from each other at least eight or nine hours a day; the wife has seen her husband for a half-hour in the morning, a few hours at night, and on weekends.

But the minister's wife has been with her husband most of his life.

The average wife has nothing much to do with herself once she has finished the household chores.

The minister's wife has so *much* to do that she seems almost never to have time for her own affairs.

On these two counts, then, the minister's wife enters retirement with advantages: she is used to having her husband around most of the time. And her schedule permits new vistas of free time which can be devoted to happy living with her husband.

But she also inherits disadvantages.

"Perhaps the hardest adjustment I had to make when my husband retired from the ministry," one woman told me, "was to face the fact that we were no longer in the center of the stage. Previously my husband and I had been the pivot about which much of our community's life moved. Now suddenly we were on the fringe of the circle, just two more members of the church."

Another woman expressed the same thought: "It takes an awful lot of grace—much more than most of us have—to sit in the pew and not think how much better the sermon would be if it were *your* husband up there in the pulpit."

The temptation to be jealous of the new minister (and

his wife) is one that can be avoided by doing what most experts on ministerial retirement suggest: moving to another town. But this, in turn, creates its own problem for the minister's wife.

"Finding and making new friends was my hardest task after my husband left his pulpit," I was told by another woman. "We moved to a strange town, and although we were welcomed there by the church circle, it was difficult to make the kind of close, good friendships we had had at home. It just seemed that most people had too much to do, too many friends, too many demands on their time to be interested in opening their hearts and minds sincerely to two more people."

Several other wives said the same thing. "It didn't matter so much to my husband," said one. "He had his projects and his hobbies, and he had never really had time before for socializing, so he didn't mind. But I was always at the center of things. I like people, and it is hard to have so few of them around."

The answer, of course, is much the same for the minister's wife as for the minister: she must seek out the advantages her husband's retirement has brought her, and the responsibilities it has brought her, and go to work with all her energies in fulfilling both.

The minister's wife can, for example, be far more of a force in the community after retirement than she was even in her function as a pastor's wife. She may not be quite so hectically busy—and this she will probably not regret. But she will have the freedom for the first time to follow her natural bent, and to follow it to the limit of her energy and ability.

This is no small thing. As a minister's wife, she was an organizer, the force behind action, the power behind the throne of so many of the church's activities. She was expected to lend her support and presence to virtually every group and function, but she was forbidden by unwritten law from becoming the recognized leader of many. And so her experience as an organizer, a get-it-done person, was built up through the years while her *leadership* qualities remained masked.

But with her husband's retirement, these qualities are free at last to burst into full flower. Her lifelong experience can now be channeled into areas of tremendous value for her community; and she herself can take her rightful place upon the stage as a leader among women.

No longer hemmed in by "what will people think if the minister's wife does thus-and-so," she can even take part in activities which were heretofore looked-upon askance—local political activity, for instance. She can play much more of a leading part in community affairs without being accused of "throwing her weight around." She can express her opinions without worrying whether she is going to cause difficulties for her husband.

She can experiment with ideas. If she has had a long-suppressed desire to paint, she can join a local art class or art club, try it and see what happens. She may produce daubs and quickly quit. Or she may produce daubs and still enjoy it; or she may even turn out to be another Grandma Moses. At any rate, she no longer has so many obstacles to enlarging her field of interests. And all this, in turn, enriches a marriage in the retirement years. A husband who sees his wife blooming with new freedom and busy with new activities has one great concern removed from his mind.

If it is useful or necessary for a wife to help out financially after retirement, there are many ways in which she can do so. (In fact, many of the projects outlined in Chapters Six and Seven are just as applicable to women as to men.) But there are also definite "women's ways" in which the minister's wife can be a contributor to the annual income.

With the real interest in people developed during her

years of active service as a minister's wife, she can logically think of doing work with children, elderly people or troubled people. Here are some examples of what other women have done:

One Cincinnati woman has developed a profitable service by running errands for hospital patients who do not have relatives and friends to help them, or who at any rate do not want to burden others with requests for this favor or that chore. She shops for cosmetics and toiletries, clothing, books and magazines; borrows and returns library books; handles correspondence; buys layettes for new mothers; and takes care of a host of other services as they arise. She charges either by the hour or on the basis of a ten percent commission on articles she buys for her clients.

Another woman accumulated a list of repairmen, craftsmen, and handymen whose services she used at one time or another, and opened a "fix-it" business with no more equipment than a telephone and a good deal of energy. She made her arrangements with the people who performed the work, then simply announced that she knew reliable and competent help. Most women would prefer to make one call to her, rather than shop around town for hours in a search for a trustworthy floor polisher or window washer. Her business was soon booming!

Many retired ministers' wives have been extremely successful working with children. Their big advantage is that other mothers trust their youngsters with them readily. Some women baby-sit, others take youngsters into their homes if parents must be away for a while. One woman serves as a "guest mother"—going into homes where illness or other emergencies have incapacitated the mother, and where several youngsters and a husband must be fed and clothed.

Many women have organized baby-sitting services, along the lines of the "fix-it" service. All you need is a telephone, a card file, a dependable group of sitters, and perhaps a postcard to send to mothers in your neighborhood, acquainting them with your service. The profit comes from a percentage of the fee.

Movie managers will welcome the woman who can control a horde of youngsters who invade their theatres for Saturday matinees. The "movie mother" merely has to patrol the aisles for a few hours and keep the enthusiasm of her charges from breaking bounds. She receives from $5 to $10 for her afternoon's work. Many communities have passed ordinances *requiring* theatres to provide such matron services.

After retirement, you and your wife will have many responsibilities toward each other—some old, some new. And you will have new responsibilities toward your children and grandchildren.

You must be prepared to understand and—if necessary—to "give way" to what you consider the younger generation. If they seem difficult and different, it is generally because *you* have become inflexible. There is more truth than jest in the old joke about the middle-aged couple who were denouncing the "younger generation" when an elderly gentleman suddenly rose to his feet and said, "Stop bothering those kids; it's you folks in the younger generation who've caused all the trouble!"

Yes, you were the "younger generation" once yourself. And it is wise to remember how you felt and acted then. It will help you in dealing with your "youngsters."

Be with them as much as possible, but not more than they want. Open your mind to their ideas, for the flow of ideas between youth and maturity strengthens both. Be tolerant of what they read and say and do. Be more than tolerant, as a matter of fact: Read and do some of it yourself. You may like it.

Interfere with your grown children as little as possible.

And don't be a second-guessing or over-indulgent grandparent.

If you must live with your children for either a short while or for a long time, consider yourself a guest in their house. This advice may hurt or upset you, but that is, after all, what you will be. At best, a welcome guest; at worst, a tolerated one. If you act with the courtesy and friendliness of a guest, family relationships will benefit.

What are a husband's responsibilities toward his wife? First, he must make every effort to protect her financially after his death. As we have seen from the life expectancy tables in an earlier chapter, women live longer than men. And since wives are generally younger than their husbands to begin with, most women must be prepared for several years of widowhood.

You can make pension, insurance and social security arrangements which guarantee a continued income for her; but above all you should leave your financial and legal affairs in good shape. You should take your wife into your confidence about them. You should leave a will, even if you do not have much property to dispose of.

Half the husbands in the U.S. die *intestate*—without a will—in the mistaken belief that what they leave will go to their wives in any event. Nothing could be more incorrect. States have varying inheritance laws. In New York State, for instance, a widow gets only one-third of an estate if there is no will, the remaining two-thirds being divided among the children.

Under these circumstances, your wife may have to sell your home; may get involved in court fights with consequent expensive legal fees; may become painfully embroiled in family arguments.

Even joint ownership of property does not excuse you from making a will. When men die intestate, jointly-owned property—even bank accounts—may be frozen by law until the probate court settles the estate. This can take months or years, and leave your widow without ready cash for necessary expenses.

The wisest thing you can do to discharge this responsibility to your wife is to consult a competent lawyer. He will advise you as to the best and most economical way of making sure your death will not leave your financial affairs in a legal tangle.

*Chapter Thirteen*

# YOU WILL NEVER REALLY RETIRE

"It has been said that life begins at forty. But with me, life begins today, and begins again every day."

That is the statement of a seventy-six-year-old retired minister. In it is the kernel of truth which applies to every retired minister: You will never really retire.

Ordination as a minister sets you apart from other men in this life. The bricklayer and the banker, the teacher and the engineer, may retire into a somnolence bounded by travel and hobbies and rest, with neither inclination nor demand that they continue to lay bricks, lend money, hold classes, or build machines.

But the minister—though officially he may leave his pastorate—has limitless opportunities, requests and needs to continue his work after retirement. His work is the betterment of mankind!

It is a task which may be approached in so many ways of God's devising that it literally never ceases. If the retired minister does nothing more than stand as a symbol of goodliness and Godliness, he is performing part of his function in life. That is why I say that you, as a minister, will never really "retire."

For many ministers, the most satisfying experience of all is the discovery that the opportunity to serve man and God is never-ending and constantly-beginning. Age has little to do with it. As Frederick Brown Harris, chaplain of the U.S. Senate, has said: "After all, what a man has done or what he is likely to do, is not glimpsed in the age numerals printed after his name."

The seventy-six-year-old minister whose philosophy was quoted at the beginning of this chapter still occasionally supplies pulpits, is right now writing a booklet of five-minute sermons, and, in his own words, "is more of a student than when I was in the seminary."

Others like him have found different ways to continue their service. Some teach adult Bible classes; some lead church discussion groups; one has turned his hobby to good use, and repairs stained-glass church windows; another is translating a hymnbook into Chinese.

I know of one retired minister who spent his remaining years in a small New England town just "going around shaking hands and being plain friendly." There was a huge turnout of people at his funeral. This man was a real success in his retirement simply because he had a gift for friendliness.

But whatever qualities these retired persons have, all of them are using, as F. J. Scribner has put it, "their mind and spirit's capacity for adjustment and resourcefulness [to] give them a rare grasp on the art of living."

Above all, religious faith in one's older years brings extra qualities of trust, dependence and peace. As Jane M. Hoey, Director of the Bureau of Public Assistance of the U.S. Social Security Administration, writes in *Housing the Aging:*

"Against the inner loneliness that comes at times to all of us. . . . there is, of course, but one protection—faith in God, our religion.

"Age is the time of all times when we have the depth of experience and wisdom to savor the deep wells of the spirit wherein lies eternal strength. Just as youth might be considered the period when joys of physical prowess reach their height, so age is the time when the philosophical and spiritual richness of life reaches its full fruition."

With his strong faith to reinforce him, the retired minister cannot but look ahead to his years of retirement with confidence and courage, secure in the knowledge that he has the greatest Guide of all to lead him along the path of the future.

*Appendix*

# SECTION ONE:
# NATIONAL POLLEN INDEX

# RAGWEED POLLEN INDEX

**Information from "Hay Fever Holiday," April 1955, compiled by Oren C. Durham, Pollen Survey Committee, American Academy of Allergy; Chief Botanist, Abbot Laboratories, North Chicago, Ill.)**

***The index figures for each community is based on three factors which directly affect individual pollen exposure: length of season, maximum aerial concentration of pollen, and total pollen catch on test slides throughout the season.***

| EXCELLENT (Pollen index below 1) | GOOD (P. I. between 1 and 5) | FAIRLY GOOD (P. I. between 5 and 10) |
|---|---|---|
| | **ALABAMA** | |
| Foley | | Mobile |
| | **ARIZONA** | |
| Grand Canyon (North Rim and South Rim—Fall only) | | Tucson (Fall) |
| Phoenix | | |
| | **CALIFORNIA** | |
| El Centro | Alpine | |
| Escondido | Arcata | |
| Lasson Volcanic National Park | Santa Barbara | |
| Los Angeles | | |
| Monterey | | |
| Oakland | | |
| Pasadena | | |
| Sacramento | | |
| San Diego | | |
| San Francisco | | |

# RAGWEED POLLEN INDEX

## CALIFORNIA (Continued)

| EXCELLENT (Pollen index below 1) | GOOD (P. I. between 1 and 5) | FAIRLY GOOD (P. I. between 5 and 10) |
|---|---|---|
| Sequoia National Park | | |
| Yosemite National Park | | |

## COLORADO

| EXCELLENT | GOOD | FAIRLY GOOD |
|---|---|---|
| Glenwood Springs | Colorado Springs | |
| Mesa Vera Nat'l Park | | |
| Pikes Peak | | |
| Estes Park | | |
| Grand Lake | | |

## FLORIDA

| EXCELLENT | GOOD | FAIRLY GOOD |
|---|---|---|
| Fort Myers | Bradenton | Clearwater |
| Key West | Coral Gables | Fort Lauderdale (Beach) |
| Miami Beach | Daytona Beach | Jacksonville |
| Pensacola (Santa Rosa Is.) | Everglades Nat'l. Park | Pensacola |
| St. Petersburg | Fort Lauderdale (Beach) | Tallahassee |
| | Fort Pierce | |
| | Live Oak | |
| | Miami | |
| | Orlando | |
| | Panama City (Sunny-side Beach) | |
| | Sebring | |
| | West Palm Beach | |

## GEORGIA

| EXCELLENT | GOOD | FAIRLY GOOD |
|---|---|---|
| | Valdosta | |

## IDAHO

| EXCELLENT | GOOD | FAIRLY GOOD |
|---|---|---|
| Moscow | Boise | |
| Sun Valley | Pocatello | |

# RAGWEED POLLEN INDEX

| EXCELLENT (Pollen index below 1) | GOOD (P. I. between 1 and 5) | FAIRLY GOOD (P. I. between 5 and 10) |
|---|---|---|
| | **MAINE** | |
| Deblois | Bar Harbor | Augusta |
| Endfield | Boothbay Harbor | Camden |
| Greenville Junction | Eagle Lake | Eastport |
| Macwahoc | Houlton | North Augusta |
| Millinocket | Jackman | Orono |
| Newagen | Lincoln | Rangeley |
| New Portland | Machias | Rockland |
| Presque Isle | Newport | Southport |
| Quoddy Head | Oquossoc | York |
| St. Francis | Spreckle Mt. | |
| | Upper Dam | |
| | **MASSACHUSETTS** | |
| | Annisquam | Magnolia |
| | East Gloucester | Nantucket Island |
| | West Gloucester | Rockport |
| | | Worcester |
| | **MICHIGAN** | |
| | Copper Harbor | Houghton |
| | Isle Royale Nat'l. Park | St. Ignace |
| | Sault Ste. Marie | |
| | **MINNESOTA** | |
| | | Tower |
| | | Virginia |
| | **MISSISSIPPI** | |
| | | Biloxi |
| | **MONTANA** | |
| Glacier National Park (Belton and Many Glacier) | Miles City | |

# RAGWEED POLLEN INDEX

## NEVADA

| EXCELLENT (Pollen index below 1) | GOOD (P. I. between 1 and 5) | FAIRLY GOOD (P. I. between 5 and 10) |
|---|---|---|
| Lake Mead, Hoover Dam (Fall) | Lake Mead, Hoover Dam (Spring) | |
| Reno | | |

## NEW HAMPSHIRE

| EXCELLENT | GOOD | FAIRLY GOOD |
|---|---|---|
| Carrol | Bath | Berlin |
| Errol | Bethlehem | Claremont |
| Laconia | Blue Job Mt. | Concord |
| Lancaster | Colebrook | Federal Hill |
| Moosilaukee | Conway | Keene |
| Pawtuckaway | Crotched Mt. | Manchester |
| | Derby | New Ipswich |
| | Dixville | Weirs |
| | Dover | |
| | Franklin | |
| | Groveton | |
| | Hampton | |
| | Hillsboro | |
| | Holderness | |
| | Lincoln | |
| | Littleton | |
| | New London | |
| | North Conway | |
| | Ossipee | |
| | Pittsburg | |
| | Plymouth | |
| | Warren | |
| | Whitefield | |

## NEW MEXICO

| EXCELLENT | GOOD | FAIRLY GOOD |
|---|---|---|
| | Roswell | Albuquerque |

## NEW YORK

| EXCELLENT | GOOD | FAIRLY GOOD |
|---|---|---|
| Blue Mountain Lake | Elk Lake | Big Moose |
| Kenne Valley | Keene | Chateaugay Lake |

# RAGWEED POLLEN INDEX

## NEW YORK (Continued)

| EXCELLENT (Pollen index below 1) | GOOD (P. I. between 1 and 5) | FAIRLY GOOD (P. I. between 5 and 10) |
|---|---|---|
| Saranac Valley | Long Lake | Chilson |
| | Loon Lake | Indian Lake |
| | Newcomb | Inlet |
| | Big Indian | Lake Placid |
| | Haines Falls | McColloms |
| | Pine Hill (Funcrest) | Owl's Head |
| | Montauk | Paul Smiths |
| | | Racquette Lake |
| | | Redford |
| | | Sabattis |
| | | Schroon Lake (Severance) |
| | | Tupper Lake |
| | | Wanakena |
| | | Fleischmanns |

## NORTH CAROLINA

| EXCELLENT | GOOD | FAIRLY GOOD |
|---|---|---|
| | Great Smoky Mountains Nat'l. Park, Newfound Gap | |

## OREGON

| EXCELLENT | GOOD | FAIRLY GOOD |
|---|---|---|
| Coquille | | |
| Crater Lake Nat'l. Park | | |
| Milton-Freewater | | |
| Portland | | |

## SOUTH DAKOTA

| EXCELLENT | GOOD | FAIRLY GOOD |
|---|---|---|
| | | Mobridge |

# RAGWEED POLLEN INDEX

| EXCELLENT (Pollen index below 1) | GOOD (P. I. between 1 and 5) | FAIRLY GOOD (P. I. between 5 and 10) |
|---|---|---|
| **TENNESSEE** | | |
| | Great Smoky Mountains Nat'l. Park, Newfound Gap | |
| **TEXAS** | | |
| | Big Spring | |
| **UTAH** | | |
| Bryce Canyon Nat'l. Park | Vernal | Salt Lake City |
| Zion National Park | | |
| **VIRGINIA** | | |
| | | Shenandoah Nat'l. Park (Big Meadows) |
| **WASHINGTON** | | |
| Mt. Rainier Nat'l. Park (Longmire Paradise Valley, White River) | | Walla Walla |
| Olympic National Park | | |
| Seattle | | |
| Spokane | | |
| Yakima | | |
| **WYOMING** | | |
| Grand Teton National Park | | |
| Yellowstone Nat'l. Park (Mammoth, West Yellowstone) | | |

# SECTION TWO: YOUR TAXES

Constant changes in the income tax laws, plus increasingly complicated income tax forms, create a double hurdle for the retired or about-to-be-retired minister. Although he may no longer draw a weekly salary, he is nevertheless likely to be receiving income from church retirement plans or pension funds. Since income from such sources falls under some of the trickiest rulings of the tax law, it can be worth many hundreds of dollars to be certain that you are receiving and reporting these funds under conditions most advantageous to you.

It is up to you and you alone to see to it that you pay no more income tax than is necessary. No one else is going to do the job for you. It is also up to you, of course, to make sure that you do not err on the other side; for even an unintentional error on a tax return may prove to be expensive and embarrassing.

### PAYMENTS RECEIVED FROM A CHURCH AFTER RETIREMENT

Retirement payments received by a minister from a church can be considered as either taxable income or as a nontaxable gift—depending first on the method by which the payments were authorized, and second on the *intent* in giving them on the part of the church organization or congregation. Therefore the taxable status of any payment received by you after retirment must be carefully checked. And preferably its status should be determined *before* you retire, to avoid problems.

The Treasury Department generally regards any payment made by an employer to a former employee as compensation. Therefore, it usually regards pension payments as taxable income to the recipient, justifying its position on the ground that the payment of the pension was contemplated "during the period of actual rendition of services and, in effect, represents compensation for such past services rather than a true gift."

The tax courts have uniformly agreed with the Treasury Department in respect to pensions paid to ministers after retirement. On appeal to the Federal Circuit Courts of Appeal, however, the position of the Treasury Department has so far been just as uniformly rejected. Today, pension amounts paid to a minister after retirement, *and decided upon at the time of retirement or after retirement,* are deemed to be non-taxable gifts rather than taxable compensation.

Really significant sums of money for the retired minister may hinge on this question; and if it is likely that your church plans to present you with a cash gift after your retirement, or hopes to continue to pay you a salary even after you have ended your active service, it is important that you understand how stormy and complex the court history of the question has been.

Let's look first at a 1949 case known as *Schall vs. Commissioner.* A minister who had served a congregation in Pennsylvania for more than eighteen years suffered a heart attack which made it necessary for him to resign and to live in Florida. He was without financial means to do so, as his congregation knew. Without any request on his part, and indeed without his knowledge, the congregation determined not only to accept his resignation, but also to pay him $2,000 a year without any pastoral authority or duties.

The minister did not agree to render any services in consideration of these payments, and, in fact, thereafter performed no pastoral services for his congregation. He testified that he regarded the payments as an outright gift.

Despite the testimony, the Tax Court held that the payments represented compensation and not a gift. However, on appeal to the United States 5th Circuit Court of Appeals, that court held that under all these circumstances there was clearly an intent to make a gift, and the fact that the resolution adopted by the congregation had characterized the payments as "salary and honorarium" did not make it a payment for services.

Although the facts were substantially similar to those present in the *Schall* case, the Tax Court nevertheless in two June, 1953, decisions held that two other retired pastors failed to show that the payments made after retirement were gifts.

In the case of *Charles S. Abernethy,* the taxpayer was a minister who retired in 1941 at the age of sixty-nine, after having served his congregation for over twenty years. Since retirement he performed no duties for the church, except that he was invited to preach once or twice a year as a guest preacher.

After retirement, the church adopted a proposal to give the pastor a lump-sum payment; and in 1944 the church further resolved to provide monthly payments for life, increasing these payments in 1947. The Tax Court held that these sums represented taxable compensation for past services and were not in the nature of gratuities. On April 1, 1954, the U. S. Court of Appeals for the District of Columbia reversed this decision.

In the case of *Andrew Mutch,* the Tax Court came to the same conclusion on similar facts. In this case the minister of the Bryn Mawr Presbyterian Church retired in 1936 after almost twenty-five years of service. Upon the recommendation of the Session of the church (its governing board for spiritual matters), the Board of Trustees passed a resolution authorizing the monthly payment of an "honorarium."

When the Commissioner of Internal Revenue claimed that such payments were taxable compensation and not a gift, the minister, to support his contention that they were gifts, relied on the testimony of the members of the Session to the effect that such payments were intended as gifts.

The Tax Court adopted the position of the Commissioner, and stated that the minister had not proved that the payments represented gifts rather than compensation. It suggested the minister's proof would have been more convincing if he had had members of the Board of Trustees, as well as members of the Session, as witnesses, and if there was evidence as to how the payments were carried on the books and records of the church. On January 13, 1954, the United States 3rd Circuit Court of Appeals reversed the decision of the Tax Court.

Another case, decided in June, 1953, involved a rabbi who had served his congregation in Detroit from 1907-1946. On September 2, 1937, the Board of Trustees of the congregation adopted a resolution providing that in the event the rabbi elected to retire, the congregation would provide an annual pension of $5,000, payable monthly, for the balance of his life. The members of the congregation adopted a similar resolution on September 23, 1937.

In 1946 the rabbi tendered his resignation, at which time the Board of Trustees adopted another resolution accepting the resignation and stating that the $5,000 retirement sum should be increased to $7,500. This resolution was ratified by the members of the congregation.

In its findings of fact the court found that the rabbi did

not request pension awards in 1937 and 1946 and that they were solely the voluntary action of the Trustees and members of the congregation. On the basis of these facts the court concluded that the resolution of 1937 resulted in a fixed legal obligation on the part of the congregation and therefore the retirement payment of $5,000 was taxable income to the rabbi.

However, the $2,500 increase at the time of retirement was a voluntary payment and did not make the congregation liable and therefore was not taxable income, but was in the nature of a gift to the rabbi. The United States Court of Appeals for the 6th Circuit affirmed the decision of a lower Federal court.

The law with respect to payments made by your church after retirement may be summarized as follows:

*1.* If your church is legally obligated to make a retirement payment to you, then such payments must be included in your taxable income.

2. If your church is not legally obligated to make retirement payments, then such payments may be excluded from your taxable income, provided there is evidence that those payments were intended as gifts and not as compensation for services rendered in the past.

If you believe that your retirement payments are in fact gifts, do not report them as part of your gross income but attach a separate explanatory statement setting forth both the amount and the fact that payments are gifts and therefore do not constitute taxable income. Be prepared to produce evidence that the payments were intended as gifts and not in consideration for past services.

### CONTRIBUTIONS TO A CHURCH PENSION FUND

The tax treatment to you of payments to a trust or life insurance company pursuant to a retirement benefit plan may depend on a number of factors, including whether the plan is qualified under the Internal Revenue Code; whether the plan provides that the church bear the entire cost; whether life insurance protection is provided in addition to retirement benefits; whether your rights under the plan are forfeitable or nonforfeitable; and whether benefits are provided by annuity contracts or in some other way.

*Qualified Plans.* If the retirement benefit plan is properly qualified under the Internal Revenue Code, then contributions by the church under it are not taxable income to you. However, where the plan requires that you contribute to your future pension along with the church, *your contribution* may not be excluded from your gross income.

Even if the pension provides for no contribution on your part, if there is provision in the plan for life insurance protection, you will be taxed in each year that the church makes a premium payment. The amount taxable is that portion of the contribution allocable to the life insurance element of the plan.

*Non-Qualified Plans.* Sometimes the church may establish a pension trust, or purchase pension annuities, pursuant to a plan which does not qualify under the Internal Revenue Code. In such cases the tax consequences to you in the year that the church makes its contribution depend on whether your rights are forfeitable or nonforfeitable.

This means that if your rights under the plan will immediately vest in the portion of the church contribution allocable to you, then that portion is taxable income to you. If your rights do not immediately vest, and can be forfeited upon termination of employment, then the amount of church contributions toward your pension is not taxable to you. If your rights under the plan are originally forfeitable but later become nonforfeitable, the contributions by the church are still not income to you.

Despite the fact that your rights under the non-qualified pension plan are nonforfeitable from its inception, you need not include the contributions in your gross income if the church which has established the pension plan, and which funds it by the purchase of annuity contracts, is a corporation exempt under Section 501 (C) of the Internal Revenue Code of 1954.

If you are in doubt as to whether your church plan is qualified, or whether your rights under a non-qualified plan are forfeitable or nonforfeitable, or whether your retirement benefit has been provided by the purchase of annunity contracts, check with church officials.

Bear in mind that *your* payments toward a plan are *not* deductible.

Make sure you understand that the *contributions* to a pension plan are *treated differently from the receipt* of pension payments.

Generally, when an employer purchases an annuity contract for an employee, the latter is taxed in the year the premium is paid, for the full amount of the premium, and again at the time of receipt of the proceeds under the contract.

However, employees of religious or charitable corporations have a tax advantage of other employees. If your church qualifies under Section 501(C) as a corporation organized exclusively for religious purposes, you can exclude the amount of the premium paid by the church from your gross income. You only pay tax on the proceeds received under the annuity contract.

An annuity contract is a contract whereby one party agrees, for a consideration, to make periodic payments to another for life; or for a guaranteed fixed period or for life, whichever is longer; or for life and a guaranteed fixed period. Installments which are merely payable for a period of years are not annuities.

The underlying theory of an annuity contract is that the money you put up with the company will be returned to you over the remainder of your life, together with the net increment representing interest which the company is able to earn by investing your money. In other words, each payment you receive is partly a return of your own money and partly income to you.

In order to include in your gross income the portion that represents interest, and in order to exclude the portion that represents the return of the cost of the annuity contract, the law prior to 1954 provided that a portion of the annuity payments received during a taxable year equal to 3% of your cost of the annuity contract was to be included in gross income, and the remainder of the annuity payments was considered a return of your cost.

The 3% rule has been completely changed by the Revenue Code of 1954. It provides that the tax-free portion of an annuity will be spread evenly over the annuitant's lifetime.

Under the new rule you are permitted to exclude each year a portion of your annuity equal to the amount paid for the annuity divided by your life expectancy. This exclusion is to remain the same even though you outlive your life expectancy. This makes it much easier to determine the taxable portion of your annuity. Your insurance or annuity company can now provide you with a statement indicating the amount which is to be taxed annually for the rest of your life.

For example, under the old rule if you purchased an annuity of $1,200 per year at a cost to yourself of $10,900, you would report as income 3% of $10,900 or $327. You would exclude the remaining $873 per year until you recovered the entire $10,900. Thereafter the entire $1,200 would be taxable.

Under the new rule, if you purchased an annuity of $1200 at a cost to yourself of $10,900 and your life expectancy when the annuity payments commence is ten years, you exclude in each year $1,090 ($10,900 divided by 10) of the $1,200 annuity and only $110 ($1,200 − $1,090) is taxable to you each year, no matter how long you live.

If you own *an annuity purchased before January 1, 1954,* the computation is made as follows: For example on January 1, 1949 if you purchased an annuity of $500 per year at a cost to yourself of $10,000, from 1949 to 1953 you should have reported as income 3% of $10,000 or $300, and you should have excluded the remaining $200 per year. You have received amounts equal to $800 toward the cost of your annuity and your unrecovered cost is $9,200. Henceforth, from and after 1954 you compute the taxable amount as if you have purchased an annuity of $500 per year at a cost to yourself of $9,200, and you calculate the amount that is tax-free and taxable in and after 1954, as described above.

If the payments are to be made over a period of years instead of for life, the annual exclusion is determined by dividing the cost by the number of annual payments. Hence, if you are to get an endowment of $1,000 over a period of ten years and the cost of your endowment policy is $9,000, you can exclude $900 ($9,000 divided by 10) and you are taxed on $100 ($1,000 − $900 per year.)

If you get a *joint and survivor annuity,* you determine your annual exclusion by dividing the cost of the contract by the combined life expectancy. For example if you bought a $15,000 annuity contract which is payable to you and your wife during your joint lives and during the life of the survivor at the rate of $1,000 a year, and your joint life expectancy is 25 years, the excluded portion of each $1,000 annuity payment is $600 ($15,000 divided by 25) and $400 is included in gross income.

If you are a recipient of a *refund annuity,* the method of computing the annual exclusion and the taxable amount is essentially the same except that you have to deduct the probable amount which is tax-free and the amount which is taxable.

### PENSION AND RETIREMENT PAYMENTS

Pension and retirement payments are treated as ordinary annuity payments where you contribute to the cost of the retirement plan, and receive such payments because of your participation in a church or other pension retirement plan.

If your pension receipts during the first three years exceed your contribution to the plan, then you are not taxed until you have recovered your total contribution after which time your entire pension will be taxed in full. For example, if you contribute $3,000 toward your pension and you get $1,200 a year at the time of retirement, the first $3,000 (the amount of your cost) is tax-free; $600 is taxable in the third year, and after that the entire $1,200 is taxable in each year that you receive a pension payment.

However, if the pension receipts in the first three years do not exceed your contribution to the plan, then the ordinary annuity rules as set forth above are applicable.

Although pensions, retirement income and annuities form the bulk of the major tax-problem situations likely to confront a retired minister, other tax questions may arise from time to time. For a thorough survey of ministerial tax problems, an excellent sourcebook is *The Minister's Federal Income Tax Guide* (Doniger & Raughley, Inc.), from which much of this material has been quoted, with permission of the publishers.

# SECTION THREE: SOURCES AND RESOURCES

This reference section has been divided into three parts: Organizations (I), Pamphlets (II), and Reference Books (III).

In the section on Organizations, important national groups are listed. These groups are not only the source of the latest information in their various fields of activity, but can also direct you to city and neighborhood units carrying on related work.

The Pamphlets section has been subdivided into lists of free or inexpensive publications on Diet and Health (A), Economics and Mental Outlook (B), and Hobbies and Travel (C).

The Reference Books section lists a variety of publications on subjects ranging from health and hobbies to travel and business information. In almost every case, the title of the book itself is a sufficient guide to its contents; the books are listed by author for your convenience in locating them at your public library.

## I. ORGANIZATIONS

Adult Education Association of the United States, 1201 Sixteenth Street, N.W., Washington, D. C.

American Association of Social Workers, One Park Avenue, New York, N. Y.

American Association of Nursing Homes, 1970 Union Avenue, Memphis, Tenn.

American Cancer Society, 47 Beaver Street, New York, N. Y.

American Diabetes Association, 1790 Broadway, New York, N. Y.

American Foundation for the Blind, 15 West 16th Street, New York, N. Y.

American Heart Association, 1775 Broadway, New York, N. Y.

American Hearing Society, 817 Fourteenth Street, N.W., Washington, D. C.

American Hospital Association, 18 East Division Street, Chicago, Ill.

American Medical Association, 535 North Dearborn Street, Chicago, Ill.

American National Red Cross, Red Cross Headquarters, Washington, D. C.

American Nurses Association, Two Park Avenue, New York, N. Y.

American Public Health Association, 1790 Broadway, New York, N. Y.

American Public Welfare Association, 1313 East 60th Street, Chicago 37, Ill.

American Social Hygiene Association, 1790 Broadway, New York, N. Y.

Arthritis and Rheumatism Foundation, 23 West 45th Street, New York, N. Y.

Commission on Chronic Illness, 615 North Wolfe Street, Baltimore, Md.

Committee on Aging and Geriatrics, U. S. Department of Health, Education and Welfare, Washington, D. C.

Community Chests and Councils of America, 345 East 46th Street, New York, N. Y.

Family Service Association of America, 192 Lexington Avenue, New York, N. Y.

Health Information Foundation, 420 Lexington Avenue, New York, N. Y.

Joint Commission on Accreditation of Hospitals, 660 North Rush Street, Chicago, Ill.

National Association of Good Will Industries, 744 North 4th Street, Milwaukee, Wis.

National Association for Mental Health, 1790 Broadway, New York, N. Y.

National Association of Registered Nursing Homes, 25 Ridgeview Avenue, White Plains, N. Y.

National Committee on the Aging, 345 East 46th Street, New York, N. Y.

National Conference of Christians and Jews, 381 Fourth Avenue, New York, N. Y.

National Council of Churches of Christ, 297 Fourth Avenue, New York, N. Y.

National Conference of Social Work, 22 West Gay Street, Columbus, O.

National Health Council, 1790 Broadway, New York, N. Y.

National Information Bureau, 205 East 42nd Street, New York, N. Y.

National Institute of Health, Section on Gerontology, Bethesda, Md.

National Legal Aid Association, 328 Main Street, Rochester, N. Y.

National Multiple Sclerosis Society, 270 Park Avenue, New York, N. Y.

National Recreation Association, 315 Fourth Avenue, New York, N. Y.

National Safety Council, 425 North Michigan Avenue, Chicago, Ill.

National Social Welfare Assembly, 345 East 46th Street, New York, N. Y.

National Society for the Prevention of Blindness, 1790 Broadway, New York, N. Y.

National Tuberculosis Association, 1790 Broadway, New York, N. Y.

Shut-In Society, 221 Lexington Avenue, New York, N. Y.

U. S. Public Health Service, Fourth Street and Independence Avenue, S. W., Washington, D. C.

## II. PAMPHLETS

Those titles marked with an asterisk (*) are United States Government publications, available from the Superintendent of Documents, Washington 25, D. C. In ordering, be sure to give the catalog number as well as the name of the pamphlet. On occasion, your Congressman will have a small supply of such pamphlets on hand which he will send you without charge, upon request. Other pamphlets—when so indicated—are available without charge from specific government departments.

### A. Diet and Health

*Aging—A Community Problem,* U. S. Department of Health, Education and Welfare, Washington, D. C. (Free)*

*Better Teeth,* Catalog No. I 16. 29:20 (Five cents)*

"Community Health Services for an Aging Population," Catalog No. FS 2.7/a: 3207 (Five cents)*

*Eating Is Fun—For Older People Too,* The American Diabetic Association, Chicago, Ill. (Free)

*Fact Book on Aging,* U. S. Department of Health, Education and Welfare, Washington, D. C. (Free)*

*Food for Older Folks,* New York City Department of Health, New York, N. Y. (Free)

*Health Is Everybody's Business,* Catalog No. FS 2.7/a: 2968 (Five cents)*

The Human Heart, Catalog No. FS 2.50:3 (Five cents)*

*Live Long and Like It,* by C. Ward Crampton. Public Affairs Committee, 22 East 38th Street, New York 16, N. Y. (Twenty-five cents)

*Physical Reconditioning,* Catalog No. D 101:11:8-294 (Sixty cents)*

*Safety For the Household,* Catalog No. C13.4:463 (Seventy-five cents)*

*What Every Person Should Know About Milk,* Catalog No. FS-2.8:150 (Five cents)*

*Your Future and You,* Metropolitan Life Insurance Company, New York, N. Y. (Free)

B. Economics and Mental Outlook

*Age Can Be an Asset,* by Ruby Murphy. Altrusa International, 332 South Michigan Avenue, Chicago 4, Ill.

*Begin Now to Enjoy Retirement,* by Ray Giles. The Mutual Benefit Life Insurance Company, Newark 1, N. J. (Free)

*Farm and Home Financial Planning,* Catalog No. A 1.38:661 (Fifteen cents)*

*Getting Ready to Retire,* by Kathryn Close. Public Affairs Committee, 22 East 38th Street, New York 16, N. Y. (Twenty-five cents)

*Guide To Family Spending,* Catalog No. A 1.38:661 (Fifteen cents)*

*How to Buy Life Insurance,* Public Affairs Committee, 22 East 38th Street, New York 16, N. Y. (Twenty-five cents)

*Looking Forward to the Later Years,* U. S. Public Health Service, Pamphlet No. 116 (Five cents)

*Mental Hygiene of Aging,* Catalog No. FS 2.7/2 3181 (Five cents)*

*Retirement: A Second Career,* Bureau of Adult Education, 23 South Pearl Street, Albany, N. Y. (Sixty cents)

*You Can Make It for Profit,* Catalog No. C1., 4:L97/9, Vol. III (Twenty cents)*

C. Hobbies and Travel

*Attracting Birds,* Catalog No. 1 1.72:1 (Ten cents)*

*Carpentry,* Catalog No. W 1.35:5-226 (Seventy-five cents)*

*Catalog of National Park Service Publications,* C35 (Free)*

*Collection and Preservation of Insects,* Catalog No. A1.38:601 (Fifteen cents)*

*Domestic Coins Manufactured by Mints of the U. S.,* Catalog No. T.28.2:C66/7/950 (Fifteen cents)*

*Fish and Shellfish of South Atlantic and Gulf Coasts,* Catalog No. 11.72:37 (Fifteen cents)*

*Growing Annual Flowering Plants,* Catalog No. A1.9:1171 (Fifteen cents)*

*Growing Fruit for Home Use,* Catalog No. A 1.9:1001/5 (Twenty cents)*

*Growing Vegetables in Town and City,* Catalog No. A1.77:7 (Twenty-five cents)*

*Guidebook of Western United States,* Catalog No. I 19.3:614 (Fifty cents)*

*Make It of Leather,* Catalog No. C18.27:190 (Fifteen cents)*

*Mobile Home Manual,* Trail-R-Club of America, P. O. Box 1376, Beverly Hills, Calif.

*National Forest Vacations,* Catalog No. A 13.2:V13/4/950 (Twenty-five cents)*

*Painting, Repairs and Utilities,* Catalog No. W1.35:5-618 (Thirty cents)*

*Recreation Areas of U. S.* (map), Catalog No. I 29.8:R-24/948 (Twenty-five cents)*

*Postage Stamps of the United States,* 1847-1953, Catalog No. P 4.10:953 (Sixty-five cents)*

*Savory Herbs—Culture and Use,* Catalog No. A1.9:1977 (Fifteen cents)*

*Trailer Park Guide,* Trailer Coach Manufacturers Association, 20 North Wacker Drive, Chicago, Ill.

*Use of Tools,* Catalog No. N17.25:T61/2/945 (Fifteen cents)*

*Woodworking and Furniture Repair,* Catalog No. W1.35:5-613 (Seventy-five cents)*

*You Can Make It,* Catalog No. C1.14:L97/9, Vol. I (Twenty cents)*

## III. REFERENCE BOOKS

Alexander, Ken. *How to Start Your Own Mail-Order Business,* Stravon, 1950

Arthur, Julietta K., *How to Help Older People,* Lippincott, 1954

Baird, Janet (editor), *These Harvest Years,* Doubleday, 1951

Blanchard, Fessenden S., *Where to Retire and How: A Comprehensive Guide,* Dodd Mead

Blair, Thomas A., *Climatology,* Prentice Hall

Bricker, William Paul, *The Complete Book of Collecting Hobbies,* Sheridan, 1951

Buckley, Joseph C., *The Retirement Handbook: A Complete Guide to Planning Your Life,* Harper, 1953

Cavan, Ruth Shonle; Burgess, Ernest W.; Havighurst, Robert J.; and Goldhamer, Herbert, *Personal Adjustment in Old Age,* Science Research Associates, 1949

Donahue, Wilma T., and Tibbitts, Clark, *Growing in the Older Years,* University of Michigan Press, 1951

Donahue, Wilma T., (editor), *Housing the Aging,* University of Michigan Press, 1954

Donahue, Wilma T., and Tibbitts, Clark, *Planning the Older Years,* University of Michigan Press, 1950

Drury, Aubrey, *How to Retire to California,* Harper, 1950

Dusenbury, George and Jane, *How to Retire to Florida,* Harper, 1954

Fink, David H., *Release From Nervous Tension,* Simon and Schuster, 1953

Ford, Norman D., *Retire Young and Start Living,* Greenlawn

Giles, Ray *How to Retire and Enjoy It,* McGraw-Hill, 1949

Giles, Ray, *Live Better After Fifty,* McGraw-Hill, 1952

Gruver, Harold B., *A Guide to Profitable Investment,* Dutton, 1950

Gumpert, Martin, *The Anatomy of Happiness,* McGraw-Hill, 1951

Howell, Trevor H., *Our Advancing Years,* Macmillan, 1954

Johnson, Wingate M., *The Years After Fifty,* McGraw-Hill

Jordan, D. F., and Willett, E. F., *Managing Personal Finances,* Prentice Hall

Kamm, Jacob O., *Investor's Handbook,* World, 1954

Knowles, Malcom S., *Informal Adult Education,* Association Press, 1953

Lasser, J. K., and Porter, Sylvia, *Managing Your Money,* Henry Holt, 1953

Lawton, George, *Aging Successfully,* Columbia University Press, 1951

Leidy, W. Philip, *A Popular Guide to Government Publications,* Columbia University Press, 1953

Lieb, William, *Outwitting Your Years,* Prentice Hall, 1951

Lurton, Douglas, *The Complete Home Book of Money-Making,* Hanover House, 1951

Manzoni, Peter, *Metalcraft for Amateurs,* Branford, 1948

Neely, H. M., *A Primer for Star-Gazers,* Harper, 1946

Ostron, Albert A., *How to Enjoy Yourself,* Dutton, 1954

Perry, Evadna K., *Crafts for Fun,* Morrow, 1940

Peters, Frazier F., *Buying a House Worth the Money,* Little Brown, 1950

Petersen, William F., *Man, Weather, Sun,* Thomas, 1948

Preston, George H., *Should I Retire?* Rinehart, 1952

Pough, Frederick H., *A Field Guide to Rocks and Minerals,* Houghton Mifflin, 1953

Pearson, Haydn S., *Profitable Country Living for Retired People,* Doubleday, 1953

Ray, Marie Baynon, *The Best Years of Your Life,* Little Brown, 1952

Scharff, Robert, *Handicraft Hobbies for Profit,* McGraw-Hill, 1952

Sapirstein, Milton R., *Emotional Security,* Crown, 1948

Schwartz, Herman S., *The Art of Relaxation,* Crowell, 1954

Scott, Edgar, *How to Lay a Nest Egg,* Winston

Shindler, John A., *How to Live 365 Days a Year,* Prentice Hall, 1955

Stieglitz, Edward J., *The Second Forty Years,* Lippincott, 1952

Solomon, Irving, *Retire and Be Happy,* Greenberg

Tibbitts, Clark, *Living Through the Older Years,* University of Michigan Press, 1949

Vischer, Adolf L., *Old Age, Its Compensations and Rewards,* Macmillan, 1948

Walker, Kenneth, *Living Your Later Years,* Oxford University Press, 1954

Washington, Lawrence, *How to Plan Your Financial Security,* McGraw-Hill, 1949

Webster, Polly, *How to Make Money at Home,* McGraw-Hill, 1949

Williams, Arthur, *Recreation for the Aging,* Association Press, 1953

Wormser, Rene, *Personal Estate Planning in a Changing World,* Simon and Schuster, 1952